by the prophet
of the earth

By the

of the

ETHNOBOTANY

L. S. M

WITH A NEW FOREWORD

University o
TUCSON

The Library
St. Mary's College of Maryland
St. Mary's City, Maryland 20686

Prophet ◀

Earth ◀

OF THE PIMA

Curtin

BY GARY PAUL NABHAN

Arizona Press ◀
ARIZONA

The Library
St. Mary's College of Maryland
St. Mary's City, Maryland 20686

About the Author

LEONORA SCOTT MUSE CURTIN had a lifelong interest in southwestern history and natural history, especially the use of plants by various ethnic groups. She was the author of numerous journal articles and four books on ethnobotany, including *Healing Herbs of the Upper Rio Grande*.

The text of *By the Prophet of the Earth* is a direct photographic reproduction of the first edition, designed by Merle Armitage and published in 1949 by the San Vicente Foundation, Willard H. Hougland, executive director, in Santa Fe, New Mexico.

Copyright 1949 by Willard Hougland

THE UNIVERSITY OF ARIZONA PRESS
First Printing 1984

Copyright © 1984
The Arizona Board of Regents
All Rights Reserved
Manufactured in the U.S.A.

Library of Congress Cataloging in Publication Data

Curtin, L. S. M. (Leonora Scott Muse)
    By the prophet of the earth.

    Reprint. Originally published: 1st ed. Santa Fe,
N.M. : San Vicente Foundation, 1949.
    Bibliography: p.
    Includes index.
    1. Pima Indians—Ethnobotany.   2. Indians of North
America—Arizona—Ethnobotany.   I. Title.
E99.P6C8 1984   305.8'97   83-24334

ISBN 0-8165-0854-2

Contents
● ● ●

8

Foreword
● ● ●

L. S. M. Curtin's ethnobotanical studies are like snapshots that record a people's connection to the environment at a particular moment in time. In the foreword of the original edition of *By the Prophet of the Earth*, anthropologist Odd S. Halseth predicted that Curtin's work would provide a historic reference point by which to evaluate general changes within a culture and specific changes in the Pima *(O'odham)* diet. He reminded us that "we do not fully understand and appreciate the relationship of diet to health...[or]... the relationship between deculturation and acculturation." Saddened by the "tin-can diet" that had begun to replace that of the ancient Pima culture by the 1940s, both Halseth and Curtin hoped the book would further encourage renewed interest in native plant foods and "their possible virtue over the new diet from the standpoint of vitamins."

A quarter of a century passed before food scientists and their collaborators empirically established the nutritional "virtues" of the ancient Piman foods discussed in this book. By that time, studies had shown that the Gila River Pima population exhibited an unusually high incidence of diabetes mellitus and other nutrition-related diseases. A dietary survey of 277 Piman women, written by National Institutes of Health and Indian Health Service workers in 1971, revealed that traditional foods made up only a small portion of most of these women's diets. The women whose diets had shifted dramatically to "tin-can" and convenience foods were obtaining less iron and magnesium than those who had kept more to the traditional diet. Although in the early 1980s researchers still could not completely explain diet change and the increase in nutrition-related disease as a simple cause-effect relationship, the early studies stimulated others which looked at the nutritive content of plant foods prepared in the traditional O'odham way.

Since 1974 there have been several articles in *Ecology of Food and Nutrition* which demonstrate that foods harvested and prepared in traditional Piman ways are nutritionally comparable or superior to the modern convenience foods that have replaced them in reservation communities. While the analyses published by Doris Calloway, Ruth Greenhouse, Harriet Kuhnlein, Charles Weber, and others emphasize mineral and protein content more than vitamins, Leonora Curtin would nevertheless be gratified to know that her hunches have been somewhat borne out. She would be further gratified to know that such information was being discussed by the Pima themselves: during the 1970s Pima professionals and paraprofessionals with the Gila River Community Division of Human Resources began encouraging the use of native foods and the control of nutrition-related diseases.

But how directly do these food issues relate back to the Piman connection with their desert and riverine environment? The availability of certain plant and animal foods certainly diminished as the Gila River and its floodplain were degraded over the years. As chronicled in Amadeo Rea's thorough treatise, *Once a River: Bird Life and Habitat Changes on the Middle Gila* (University of Arizona Press, 1983), the Pima witnessed the decline in abundance of local flora and fauna as streamflows were diverted, groundwater pumped, soils salted up and vegetative cover cleared. Overgrazing, woodcutting, beaver trapping and inappropriate intensities of land use promoted by Spanish and Anglo settlers began to take their toll on the health of the Gila watershed after the middle of the nineteenth century. By 1887 Anglo settlers at Florence had built an irrigation system large enough to take the entire flow out of the Gila before it even reached the Pima.

The Gila River and its tributaries, the Santa Cruz and the

Salt, surely did not dry up and die all at once. Neither did Piman knowledge of these once diverse biological communities. There remained among the elderly people who call themselves the Akimel O'odham, "Running Wash People," a vivid sense of farming and gathering along a dynamic river. The Coolidge Dam did not bring "the promised new life to Pima agriculture" as anticipated in Curtin's time, nor did groundwater-based agriculture regenerate the diversity of resources that Pimans once had to draw upon. In the 1980s Piman craftsmen often had to search off the reservation to find raw materials from plants that were abundant there during their childhoods. Some sowed seed or planted cuttings of species that were formerly ubiquitous. In these ways, Piman usage of vegetation was not abandoned; it shifted, as new technologies interacted with the people's needs and skills. For this reason, we still have much to learn from native plant experts in the Gila River Indian community; it is hoped that future ethnobotanical "snapshots" will be taken with the the accuracy and timeliness of Curtin's vignettes.

In 1983 many of Curtin's field notes and manuscripts concerning the Pima, "Purepecha" Tarascans, and other Native American peoples were placed in the Special Collections archives of the University of Arizona Library. In addition, her dried plant specimens, fortunately saved over the decades by the foresight of the Pueblo Grande Museum in Phoenix, were transferred to the University of Arizona Herbarium. These primary materials, including those for this book, will thus be available for future researchers who wish to study the contributions of Curtin and her Piman consultants. The value of the research conducted for the writing of *By the Prophet of the Earth* can only grow richer as time goes on.

A final note: the title *By the Prophet of the Earth* is a reference to the abundance of nature provided for the people by the O'odham deity *Jewed Makai*, who is significant in Piman creation stories. The name of this mythic character comes from the O'odham terms *jewed* (earth, soil, land, territory, world

11

or homeland) and *makai* (medicine man, shaman, curer, seer or prophet). The name has elsewhere been translated as "Earthmaker," "Earthdoctor," or "Medicine Man of the World." In modern times the phrase has also been used for Anglo doctors, and Madeleine Mathiot's *A Dictionary of Papago Usage* (Indiana University Publications, 1973) lists another meaning for *jewed makai*, "land surveyor"—a telling reflection of the way some O'odham view the changing of their modern world.

GARY PAUL NABHAN

Introduction
● ● ●

Because he knew of my love for primitive people and of the great joy I had found working with them in New Mexico and Morocco, Mr. Odd S. Halseth, Director of Pueblo Grande Laboratory of Phoenix, urged me to record the ethnobotany of the Pima Indians while there was still the opportunity. Other researchers maintained that the ancient culture of the Pima had been absorbed in the process of modernization of the Indian, but Mr. Halseth insisted that there still lived on the reservation enough old people with a knowledge of the past to make such a record possible.

The rough going of the first of my four seasons in the Pima field was made smoother through the kindly and capable offices of Miss Elizabeth Hart, for seven years engaged in home extension work on the reservations. I accompanied Miss Hart on her daily visits to the Indian women's clubs, and while she was occupied in teaching domestic science, I wandered about the countryside collecting plants on which the women gave me information after the teaching session. Always it was the older women who had the greatest knowledge of the native uses of plants. Those of middle age would occasionally supply a recipe, but girls of high-school age would have no answer when questioned. Some medicinal plants are recognized by all the Pima, while others are known only to certain individuals. It was also found that, in many instances, Papago, Apache, Yaqui, and Maricopa also used or knew of certain Pima plants.

Miss Hart was particularly interested in my work because she had herself collected data on the plants formerly used for food by the Pima. She constantly urged the Indians to grind their home-grown grain instead of buying at the store white flour lacking in both vitamins and bulk. In several instances I have quoted from her various booklets, now out of print. Stephen Jones explained to me that in the seventies, when the water situation became acute, the Pima were starving because they could no longer grow wheat, hence they were forced to return to their wild foods for sustenance. This is the reason why the old people still remembered the original food that nature gave them. They constantly complained that most of their edible greens have disappeared, and no wonder, for, owing to the white man's draining of the water supply for his own irrigation, the shallow wells of the Pima became exhausted, necessitating the hauling of water in barrels for household use either from trading posts or from the schools.

During the succeeding three seasons when I went out alone, I invariably received the friendliest cooperation, one informant or interpreter introducing me to another, but carefully warning me against those who might not be persuaded to talk or who might invent tales in order to evade the truth.

I was astonished when a white woman, who had spent many years of her life in Phoenix, told me that she feared even to speak to a Pima, as "they are so black and look so surly." On the contrary, I have found them good-natured and kind. When among friends they display an attitude like that of happy, normal children. Their sense of humor is so delightful that I have endeavored in this work to present a slight taste of it. Witness, for example, Lewis Manuel's explanation of why his ancestors were thin, and old Mary Manuel's continuous flow of witty conversation. Here and there, in the hope of giving a bit of characteristic flavor, I have set down the exact words as they came from my informants' lips.

The following citations from earlier choniclers show that the character of the Pima has not changed for generations:

According to Bartlett (vol. II, p. 267) Father Kino, in 1698, comments on the "peacefulness and gentleness" of these Indians and remarks on their irrigated lands and cultivated fields of wheat.

Emory often mentions the merry jokes of the "Pimos," and praises them for their agriculture and useful arts, describing them as peace-loving and industrious.

Bartlett, (vol. II, p. 264) wrote: "There are no tribes of Indians on the continent of North America more deserving of the attention of philanthropists than those of which I am speaking. None have ever been found further advanced in the arts and habits of civilized life. None exhibit a more peaceful disposition, or greater simplicity of character; and certainly none excel them in virtue and honesty. They are quite as industrious as their necessities require them to be."

Owing to faulty modern diet, the Pima tend to obesity at middle age, so that their exceedingly small feet seem inadequate to support their rotund bodies. The intense desert sun burns them almost black, hence they are much darker than, for example, the Pueblo Indians of New Mexico. In fact, the appellation "red-skin" is hardly appropriate, although there is no suggestion of the negroid about them.

Thanks to an excellent hospital at Phoenix, Pima medicine-men have largely passed out of fashion. A generation ago, the lives of the native healers were in great danger because tribal laws prescribed that if a patient were allowed to die, they were killed. (See Russell, pp. 42, 48.)

As with most primitive people, weights and measures are almost unknown. Time is not an important factor in their lives. Science may demand more specific prescriptions or recipes, but the Pima give only these indefinite directions: "A pinch or a handful in a little or a lot of water and allowed to steep or boil until the liquid is light- or dark-brown." From their point of view there is nothing more to be said; and perhaps, after all, it matters little, for in most cases such prescriptions do not involve powerful drugs.

Spring was a favorable season for field research, as the countryside was carpeted with flowers. Even if the Indians were engaged in planting, with a little patience, extended inquiry, and an hour or so of search, an informant would be found and at least an appointment could be made. But during the autumn, when all vegetation had become shriveled, every Pima under ninety years became busy in picking cotton for the whites. Although my speedometer might register two hundred miles a day, my notebook often remained blank. Human contacts, warm, friendly, amusing, and touching experiences were mine. Above all, the desert in its varying moods ever brought delight, so that each day was crowned by a glorious sunset. Even the plants along the roadside repeated their own stories, and I never felt lonely driving through the Indian country. Moreover, the roadrunner kept me company, always scurrying along beside the car and welcoming as lucky the days of our meeting.

Had the advent of war not terminated my field research, doubtless more legends and beliefs would have been entrusted to my ear. It was only during my fourth and last season that sufficient friendliness and confidence were established for such intimate, well-guarded secrets to be shared.

L. S. M. CURTIN

Acknowledgments
● ● ●

Since I am not a trained botanist, I turned to Mr. Robert H. Peebles, Agronomist at Salt River Experimental Station and co-author of "Flowering Plants and Ferns of Arizona," published by the U. S. Department of Agriculture, Washington, 1942. Mr. Peebles was of invaluable assistance in identifying my specimens, which are deposited with the Pueblo Grande Laboratory in Phoenix, and in cooperating in every way possible, even to the extent of giving me some of his findings on local plant usage, as well as other scientific knowledge.

Mr. Odd S. Halseth took many trips into the field with me during my four seasons of research, and his understanding of the Indians, combined with their affection for him, greatly facilitated the collection of data.

Dr. Frederick W. Hodge of the Southwest Museum, Los Angeles, has always shown an encouraging enthusiasm for all the ethnobotanical work that I have done, and to him I am deeply grateful.

Such kindness as that of Father Antonine Willenbrink, O.F.M., and Miss Elizabeth Hart, both mentioned elsewhere, is seldom encountered. Without them my work would have been infinitely more difficult.

To Mr. A. E. Robinson, Superintendent of the Pima Indian Agency at Sacaton, I am indebted for a letter of introduction and for his generous assistance in supplying reliable interpreters. Also to Mr. Frank Shannon, Superintendent of the Day School at Salt River Reservation, and to all the day-school superintendents, I extend hearty thanks for their aid.

Above all, I shall ever be thankful to the many Indians whose gentle and patient help made this book possible.

L. S. M. C.

Phonetics
● ● ●

Scattered as they are over the reservations, the Pima Indians pronounce their words quite differently in the various areas which they occupy, hence the district of each man can be determined by his dialect. Linguistic variations over such a short distance as that between St. John's Mission and the north bank of the Gila proved to be so much of a handicap in recording the Pima names of plants that I was forced to confine myself to the use of a single dialect. An educated Pima once told me that he had tried to read Rev. C. H. Cook's Pima translation of the Lord's Prayer, but could make "neither head nor tail of it," nor could he understand Russell's manner of writing Pima words in his monograph on the Pima Indians published in the 26th Annual Report of the Bureau of American Ethnology, 1904-05.

Although the simplified system of phonetics here employed may not meet the approbation of philologists, yet I feel justified in following that system which has been successfully used by Father Willenbrink in his "Notes on the Pima Indian Language," published in 1935 by the Franciscan Fathers of California. Father Willenbrink states that his pronunciation key is practical rather than technically scientific, and I have found it to be such in recording for ultimate printing. A number of Indians have stated to me that the Father is the only white man who speaks their language so perfectly as to be indistinguishable from that of a native Pima; and they also say that "he knows more about our grammar than we do ourselves."

It therefore seems obvious that the simplified phonetic system devised by Father Willenbrink should serve every practical purpose in recording terms and thereby obviating the necessity of employing diacritical marks and other devices which, especially to the non-professional student, are often confusing.

Father Willenbrink gave much of his valuable time in patiently checking every Pima word contained in this work; and George Webb, born at Gila Crossing of pure Indian stock and educated at Phoenix Indian School and the local High School, was frequently consulted on correct pronunciation.

The language of the Pima and Papago is remotely related to Aztec, or Nahuatl. Accent is always on the first syllable of a Pima word.

With the kind permission of Father Willenbrink I am including the following key to Pima pronunciation.

a as in papa; e.g. *babat,* frog
e as in pet; e.g. *peap,* bad
i as in pit; e.g. *itdam,* upon
o as in won; e.g. *vonam,* hat
u as in put; e.g. *choikut,* cane
ai as in aisle; e.g. *vaila,* dance
aw as in saw; e.g. *awk,* father
ee as in eel; e.g. *eebdak,* heart
oe as *u* in urn; e.g. *hoeg,* the
oi as in oil; e.g. *hoipat,* needle
oo as in moon; e.g. *oos,* stick
ue as in German *ü;* e.g. *chuet,* in
d' denotes soft *t* sound
final *khi* is used for soft *k*
kw as *qu* in quail
l similar to *lh* sound
final *phi* denotes soft *p* sound
sh not sharp as in English
yi approaches a softly aspirated *vi;* e.g. *cofyi,* woman
h preceded by *k, s, t,* is silent
ny as in canyon

The other consonants are pronounced as in English, except that *g* is always hard, as in get.

Double vowels that do not form diphthongs are indicated by a hyphen instead of the dieresis; e.g. *a-alh,* children.

Informants
● ● ●

(Unless otherwise indicated, the informants are Pima Indians.)

Mrs. Ruby Allen lives at Wetcamp.

Mrs. Elsie L. Andrews is a young and very intelligent person who is secretary of the Women's Club at Lehi.

Lizzie Anton lives at Sweetwater, Snaketown area, and is more than eighty years of age. She was born under Snake Hill during the great flood, and she remembers the flood (from which so many historical events are dated) that carried away the government mill, even though she was just a little girl at the time. She makes household baskets, storage baskets, and ollas.

Domingo Blackwater is quite a character who lives at Sacaton. Born in Blackwater nearly sixty years ago, he belongs to the Coyote clan. When I related to him a legend, he gave me several others in return. I shall always regret that we had only one interview, because he has a large store of information and is willing to share it. He told me the following story of how his grandfather got his English name: When the boy was first taken to school and asked his Indian name, he answered,

"Wihom" ('lightning man' or 'thunder'). The teacher replied, "Oh, yes, William; and from where do you come?" "Blackwater," answered the youngster: "Yes, yes, William Blackwater," said the teacher, and so it was. (See Russell, p. 18n.)

Pablo B. Chaigo at St. Anthony's Catholic Church, Sacaton, was recommended to me as interpreter by Father Antonine. Chaigo is middle-aged, with many responsibilities which he takes very seriously. Spending six days a week in visiting outlying missions, he is difficult to find at his home, which is situated back of St. Anthony's. It was Pablo who introduced me to Tashquent, who he thought would be the best informant because of his advanced age. Pablo's wife accompanied us on our second search for information and I found her very cooperative.

Mrs. Catherine Clark is a club member on Salt River Reservation, and her aged mother, Mrs. Sara Emerson, with whom she lives, makes baskets of split willow, devil's claw, and cattail.

Charlie and Stella Conger at Salt River are a very old couple, still industrious and living under the irrigation ditch which enables them to grow corn and beans.

Teresa Conger, a comparatively young Papago woman, moved to the Salt River Reservation when she was about eight years of age. She learned to make baskets from the Pima and explained with great pride her method of making coiled basketry.

Mr. Charles B. Fleming, Jr., an anglo, is head of the Botanical Laboratory at Phoenix.

Mrs. Elita Fulwiler is president of the Women's Club at Lehi. She is a bright, lively, helpful young woman, with a number of small children.

Ollie Goka, an Apache, is a very bright young woman of light complexion who lives at Fort McDowell Indian Reservation. She wore a very full calico skirt trimmed with rickrack and topped by an over-blouse fastened with large pearl buttons.

Mrs. Meta Goodwin, who lives near Salt River Day School, is an elderly woman and was at one time a famous basket-maker. Rheumatism, probably induced by years of handling the wet raw materials, forced her to relinquish her craft.

Miss Elizabeth Hart, an anglo, engaged in extension work at Fort McDowell, Salt River, Gila River, and Ak Chin Reservations, drove me all over the country and introduced me to informants.

Mrs. Barbara Harvey, a very dark woman of middle age, lives at Sacate and attends the Women's Club at South Casa Blanca. She told me that I would be welcome at any time, but, unfortunately, I was prevented from visiting her Club.

Eunice Head lives at Co-op and, as she speaks no English, I was obliged to call on Emma Howard to interpret for me. Eunice seemed very aged and suffered greatly from arthritis, for which she uses the charcoal-burning remedy. On one occasion when I called on her, she appeared to be embarrassed and cut short our interview because she had her hair plastered with black mud in preparation for a shampoo.

Paul Head, Eunice's late husband, was well informed on Pima history and had a calendar stick which was buried with him. Charles Allison, who lives at Co-op, copied the stick and can recite the history indicated by the mnemonic symbols marked thereon. Every effort was made to interview this man, but he had a steady job on the Reservation and, to my regret, I never met him. Dr. Russell (pp. 36-37, 104-105) gave a good account of the calendar stick.

José Henry lives alone in the last native roundhouse on the Salt River Reservation. He is very dark, has long wavy hair, straight short teeth, large chest and stomach, and his skin is of the same grey-black color and texture as that of water buffalo, but the occasional hairs are missing.

When a boy, José was sent to Carlisle School in Pennsylvania, but, not liking the school, he escaped and walked all the way back to the Reservation where he lived with his mother until her death. He was never married. He claims that his knowledge of medicinal plants is slight, as his health has always been excellent; besides, he said, "looking after the sick is women's business."

José allowed us to photograph his house, which he is obliged to enter while lying on his back, because his abdomen does not permit him to crawl through the narrow opening that serves as a doorway. Nothing would induce him to pose for a picture; he simply excused himself with dignity, saying that he owned no shirt. Indeed, his entire wardrobe consisted of blue overalls and sandals made from pieces of old innertube tied on with a string.

Our host showed us with pride an unfinished bow with arrow, secreted in the thatch of the ramada, which he said he must finish some day. On my first visit I noticed a wretched Rosinante which leaned against a barbed-wire fence for support, and on my return I asked for the horse and was told that she had died that very morning. It was then two o'clock in the afternoon, yet I found José sitting in the sun, scratching his chest, although he intended to "dig a deep hole" before night. When I suggested it would be well for him to hasten, lest the big birds would gather, he answered, "O, no! The big black birds have gone to the mountains for the winter." The only cloud in his life was the loss of a pet rattlesnake which he had owned for several years. He told me that one day while he was away from home a friend entered his house and killed the rattler. Indignantly, José assured me that his snake was much more of a gentleman than friend Indian!

I was impressed here in the wilderness by the fact that I had met the most contented man living, yet his primitive obscured roundhouse was only seven miles from a luxurious dude ranch where the guests exhaust themselves chasing that elusive "bluebird." An Indian guide was required for both my visits to José, because on leaving the highway numerous winding wood-roads, indistinguishable to a white person's eye, branch off in every direction and stunted trees along the river-bank obstructed the view.

Mrs. Emma Howard, president of the Women's Club, is alert, intelligent, and has a remarkably light complexion for a Pima. She happily stated that she had the best husband in the world, that he is kind and thoughtful, and neither gambles nor drinks. His face confirms her claim. She lives near Co-op (which derived its name from Co-operative, as the community was started with this idea) in a two-room adobe house with a slanting, shingled roof. Her possessions included an upright piano, a radio, a sewing machine, and Russell's book on the Pima, which she procured from Washington. She is the mother of half a dozen children, but always found time to give information and even accompanied me about the country as interpreter. Her mother and her stepfather, Mason McAffee, live a few hundred yards away in a Pima house of the old style. Her own father's name was U. S. Grant.

Isaac Howard, fifty years of age, of pure Pima blood, lives near Sacate. Isaac was a mine of information, and several times George Webb led me by long and rough roads to the Howard place, but I met him only once, as he was away making the family's meager living by hauling wood.

Isaac's complete faith in his elaborate cures, his wild-looking countenance, and the fanatical light in his eyes led me to suspect him of being a modern medicine-man. His mother, Lucy Howard, who is about eighty, also gave information. James, the father, is almost blind, and has long, gnarled thumbnails. The family is Presbyterian.

Juana Innes and Sarah Smith, Pimas, live on the Salt River Reservation and are both in their eighties. They have prepared and eaten all the plants mentioned by them, but now they are supplied with food by the Government. They seemed more interested in food-plants than in those for medicine.

Lena and John Innes are a middle-age couple. John works for the power company, tending his land and chickens on his days off. They live at Lehi in a gabled house surrounded by tall trees; and as water for irrigation is available, they cultivate a good vegetable garden. John owns a truck, and the couple seemed quite prosperous.

Edward Jackson, known as "The Colonel," is both blacksmith and iceman at Sacaton.

Mrs. Jackson lives at St. John's Mission, is unusually bright, is educated above the average, and was always ready to supply information. Her father, named Chief Anton Nanamul, was about eighty years of age, had been chief of the Catholic Pima for forty years, and is a descendant of Chief Antonio Azul, a famous character mentioned by Russell (p. 196) and by a number of Americans who passed through the Pima country from the 1840's onward. Anton was sweeping the yard around the house when I visited him, and his daughter explained, "That's all he's good for now." This seems to be the work assigned to the oldest men. Chief Anton shows his social and cultural "advancement'" by wearing false teeth and spectacles. His mind seemed to wander, and although I tried several times to procure information from him, he gave me none.

Many Pima yards are tidy, but others are littered with the accumulation of years: baby carriages, toys, discarded tires, pots, kettles and pans, rags, bottles, cans, and especially old shoes. Frequently the yards were strewn with broken-down automobiles which the children used for play and their elders enjoyed as easy chairs; but after Pearl Harbor the ancient wrecks were sold for war purposes.

Mrs. Erilie Jones, at Fort McDowell, is an Apache married to the Indian minister.

Stephen Jones, a Pima on the Salt River Reservation, asserted that he was 103 years of age and that he was born at Wetcamp (Shook*) at the time of the last fight between the Yuma and Maricopa at Gila Crossing. The Maricopa had asked the Pima for help, and all the Yuma were killed but one, who returned to his people with news of the disaster.

---

* The Indians defined this word as 'swampy place' and Father Antonine further explains that it really means 'filled up' usually with a liquid, and that any district which becomes very wet and muddy is called *shootkam jievut.*

According to Russell (p. 47) this fight took place in 1857, hence Stephen Jones was only eighty-four years of age at the time of my visit in 1941. I found that most old Indians add ten or twenty years to their age. Stephen remembered when a Government mill south of Sacaton Agency was burned, and he recalled having worked on the Wetcamp Canal, and believed that he was twenty years of age when a flood washed away the earlier mill at Casa Blanca. Stephen was baptized when a grown man by Rev. C. H. Cook, who opened a Government school at Sacaton in 1871. He maintained that he was much older than Tashquent, but he knew a more aged Pima named Koeli, which means 'old man.' This Koeli lived with his son, Enos Lyons, at Wetcamp, and although I made every effort to meet him, I was warned that it would be useless, because he was bedridden and senile.

When my informant became of age, two native hairdressers twisted the long strands on each side of his head, and very many years later a Papago cut off Stephen's hair, which reached his waist. When the strands were thrown in front of him, he confessed that he almost cried.

Nicknames are known to most of the Pima, but are seldom revealed to white people, and, naturally, are never used by the owners of the names. Stephen's nickname was *Shaw-aw-doggeda* ('one who makes faces at someone'), because many years ago, while chopping wood, he was blinded in one eye by a splinter. Now the other eye is almost sightless, but in spite of this handicap he continues to chop wood, does other chores, and goes about with the aid of a cane made from wild tamarix, inspecting the fences surrounding his place.

Lewis Manuel served as my interpreter and accompanied me several times to Stephen Jones who was his wife's grandfather. From him I collected much information, including a number of legends.

Jumbi Juan's family came from Gila River, but he was born at Lehi and first saw light in February or March at the time of the initial planting of wheat. He knows no other date. His long hair is iron-grey, and his earlocks are pure white, which make him resemble a marmoset. Jumbi Juan asserted that he never went anywhere, never joined in a game, and that all he knows is work.

Juan Leonard: Truant officer at Salt River Reservation School.

May Makil, the daughter of old Mary Manuel, lives at Lehi and her daughter Malinda attends school at Salt River. Both of her parents were Maricopa, and her husband, Juan, who never had time to give information, is Pima.

Mrs. Juanita Manuel lives at Sacaton Flats.

Lewis Manuel, a Pima, born at Blackwater and living on the Salt River Reservation at the time of my visit, believed that he was about fifty-six years of age, but did not know exactly. As his father, grandfather, and uncle were medicine-men, Lewis planned to follow the profession, but missionaries interfered and he became a jailer instead. While serving in that capacity, he was permitted to have all the prison food that he could consume. This was explained by the gesture of rubbing his fat stomach. He further stated: "In the olden days the Pima ate little—just enough—and never got fat. Because they were thin, they could run away from the Apache and after them as well." (See Bartlett, vol. II, p. 229.) After moving to Salt River Reservation Lewis was given the position of policeman. He is now official interpreter, but finds time to cultivate his land. He recounted that the aforesaid uncle was well paid with cattle for his services as medicine-man and acquired a large herd, but he "got religion" and let the animals go, confessing to his tribesmen that he had obtained them by cheating his patients and by unfair practices.

Lewis stated that while he could read, he never took advantage of this accomplishment, as reading put new ideas into his head, whereas he preferred to think of the old things and ways.

When I arrived at Lewis' house, he seated me under the ramada and insisted on telling me about his marital troubles.

He first married a girl who had been educated in the Phoenix Indian School and who spent her time reading love-story magazines which he had to buy for her every time he drove to town and for which he paid up to twenty-five cents apiece! He warned his wife that she would come to no good end, and after several years he discovered that she was unfaithful to him. He carefully thought things over and finally said to her, "You are a good Mormon and I am nothing; if I will be baptized and live according to your faith and its laws, will you do the same?" That is how it worked out, but three years later she burst her bladder ("I don't know how") and died. Now he has a young second wife.

Lewis then related the well-known story of when the whites first settled Phoenix and how they told the Indians that it was a sin to go naked, therefore, the Pima used to ride to the outskirts of town with their trousers under their arms, tether their horses, dress, and attend to their errands. When leaving, they removed their trousers for the ride home. "Now-a-days," Lewis remarked with great disgust, "white women go about half-naked and that is the correct thing to do! How can anybody but God say what is right or wrong?" There is a local ordinance, which has never been repealed, pertaining to all Indians, but was mainly for the benefit of the Maricopa and the Pima.* Another statement is that they had a community wardrobe hanging on some bushes at the old city limits, changing as they entered town or returned to the reservation.

"When the whites first came," said Lewis Manuel, "they would ask many questions, and the Indians would answer *pimatc,* meaning 'I do not know.' That is how they got the name 'Pima'." (See Russell, p. 19)

Mary Manuel, who claimed to be ninety-eight years of age, was a Maricopa. Her ancestors came down the Colorado River

* Section 13 of Ordinance No. 100 (O.S.)
Any Indian who shall appear or remain within the City of Phoenix without sufficient clothing to cover his or her person, and any Indian who shall remain within the city limits after sundown, unless in the employ of some inhabitant of the city, shall be deemed guilty of a misdemeanor.
(Passed: December 17, 1889)

and settled where Parker now is. She lived at Sweetwater, but her grandfather was moved with all his children to Fort McDowell. She had no contact with the Pima until she had reached the age of twelve and attended Dr. Cook's school where many young girls married Pima boys; but she "had no chance," she said, so thought she must have been very ugly. Nevertheless, when she moved to Lehi she met a man of her own tribe who thought her "the cutest thing he had ever seen," and married her.

Mary had always lived in a native roundhouse, the last one of which was the most easterly on the reservation, which she left twenty years ago. I found her in a windowless hut, sitting on the floor where she spent her days cooking one course of mushy food after another on a tripod-grate *(chueto)*, over a small wood fire. The only exit for the smoke was by the door. and she complained bitterly of her swollen eyelids. During the first hour in her hut, my eyes were smarting, and for two days I suffered from the effects of my visit.

Mary wore a kind of pompadour with bangs cut to the level of her eyebrows; the rest of her iron-grey hair hung loose down her back. She was doubled completely over at the waist, and when she walked it was necessary for her to use a cane in one hand while being led by a four-year-old great granddaughter. In spite of being almost blind, Mary still made pottery. She had learned to read and write, and she also knew some Spanish. Her house was situated in the Catholic Church compound.

On my second visit, accompanied by Ida Redbird whom I had brought from the Maricopa Reservation as interpreter, I gave Mary coffee and sugar, whereupon she said, "That comes in handy for a rainy day, as I am not able to get out and provide for myself." She regretted that it had been so dry that she had no plants, such as she usually collected for food, to show me. "I am still living, you see, because I have always used my native food. If our Creator would send more rain, there would be more plants for me and I would live longer. He gave us certain plants to use, and He gave us knowledge of how to

STEPHEN JONES

TASHQUENT

prepare them for food and medicine. All Indians fed on the same kinds of food, but prepared them differently; and the medicines were the same, from the same plants. Nowadays the Pima add chile, onions, etc., to their food, and the young girls complain about insufficient milk and about failing health. They eat nothing but white man's food, take his medicine, and go to the hospital; but if they had used their own herbs for various sicknesses they would have got along all right."

After four hours of inquiry, I expressed fear of having fatigued her, whereupon she answered, "O, no!" I'm only too glad to talk—I never thought of being tired. We in here are having all the fun; she who waits outside is the tired one" (referring to a friend of mine who had come along for the trip). When I asked Mary's permission to return, she said, "You will have to hurry, for I might be dead."

On revisiting the scene the following season, I found, to my sorrow, that the house had been burned, except for the large uprights and beams which had been saved because they have become so scarce. May Makil told me that her mother had died on February 16, 1941, at the age of eighty-four.

Dr. Eric Stone states that "among the Apache, Pima and Ute the hut and all the property of the patient were burned as soon as he died." (See also Russell, p. 194.)

To prove the incredible memory that these illiterate people have, I will quote Gladys Manuel, wife of Lewis. When a child she often visited Santa Cruz where lived an old Pima who kept a book with events depicted in pictures which had been drawn in pencil to be colored. Although blind, the old man explained the meanings of the pictures as records of historical occurrences, as was done in the case of the calendar stick. "In spite of his sightless state," Gladys said, "he busied himself with quilting."

Mason McAffee, who said that his "Indian name" was José Juan, was born in Sacate and was living in an old-style Pima house at Co-op. He stated that he was twelve or thirteen years of age when the first Government flourmill at Casa Blanca was washed away by flood. He remembered this incident perfectly, and stated that he had reached ninety years, but believed that Stephen Jones at Salt River is much older. When a grown man he was tattooed; his teeth, which he claimed he kept in good condition by merely wiping them with a cloth, were excellent for a man of his age; his ears were pierced, and his grey hair had been cut short when he became a Christian, for at that time Dr. Cook told him that long hair was a sinful vanity. Mrs. Emma Howard, his stepdaughter, suggested that it might have been cut for hygienic reasons.

Many of the Pima have brown stains and soft white marks on their teeth, caused by flourine in the water. Some of them rub teeth so affected with charcoal and claim beneficial results.

Dean McArthur, of the Co-operative Colony, a full-blood Pima from Sacaton, thought that he was about seventy-eight years of age; he was almost blind, and stated that he was related to Emma Howard, my interpreter. When, at the end of our interview, I thanked him for giving me such careful descriptions of the games, and asked if I might come again, he answered, "It has been a pleasure, and I will always be glad to tell you what little I know."

On leaving, I mentioned the coincidence of McArthur and Curtin having a powwow. This was much appreciated by Emma Howard, who had just heard over the radio of the meeting between General MacArthur and Prime Minister Curtin of Australia.

Lena Meskeer is a Pima from Gila Crossing who settled on the Maricopa Reservation when she married a Maricopa at the age of sixteen or eighteen. She was about seventy-two years of age at the time of my visit in 1941.

Lewis Nelson, who lives on the Salt River Reservation, was born at Blackwater in February, 1871. This month is indicated on calendar sticks as *Aupa ivakedak mashat,* meaning 'when the cottonwood leaves begin to show.' Lewis is a small man, with rather light complexion and massive brow, who speaks better average English than most of the Pima. He had been a teacher at Keam's Canyon, Arizona.

Pelvin Newman, who lived on the Sacaton Reservation, was sixty-six years of age, and attended the Presbyterian Mission School at Tucson. He makes ladles, mixing bowls, and rolling pins, and is well known throughout the reservations. Few of these craftsmen are left, as commercial articles have replaced those made in the native fashion.

Mrs. Jane Pablo lives at Wetcamp. Her neat house, which is used by the Women's Club, has a very good example of an outdoor kitchen. The place is surrounded by tall tamarix trees which the owners intended to cut down, because, they say, nothing can be grown beneath them.

Ida Redbird, a tall and exceptionally handsome Maricopa, is well informed on medicinal plants and is one of the two best potters on the Maricopa Reservation; indeed her pottery is of surpassing excellence in design and finish, and invariably wins prizes at exhibitions.

Walter Rhodes, extension worker at the Santa Cruz Day School, is an intelligent man and speaks fluent English, but his services are difficult to procure as he is extremely busy.

Angel Sánchez: I interviewed this Mexican, who lives in a little settlement near Phoenix, to check on Indian and Mexican uses of plants in that locality. Unfortunately most of the plants he described came from the high mountains, hence I have included only two or three in this work. Angel said: "God has given us many plants. Some are bad, but most of them are good for us, only we don't know all of them." He stated that he would be ninety-one years of age in August, 1941. Born in Guaymas, Sonora, he went to California, at the age of eleven, in 1862, but had lived in Arizona for sixty-five years, according to his own inconsistent statement. He mentioned that when he arrived in southern Arizona there was no Phoenix and no Prescott. He had done three kinds of work all his life: he labored in the mines, chopped wood, and boasted that everyone knew him when he broke horses.

Tashquent means 'sun count,' that is, as explained by the Indians, 'to count the days as the clock does.' This Pima informant asserted that he was ninety-five years of age and was born at Gila Crossing about the time a man named White, Agent for the Pima, started to make trouble. The Pima went to see if the agent were man enough to fight them, "but a bunch of white men came and took him away," (Russell, p. 48 dates this event, as recorded on a calendar stick, in 1861-62, which would make Tashquent only eight years of age.) However, records tell us that Ammie M. White was a trader, and well liked, when he was captured by the Confederate soldiers in 1861. He later returned to the reservation and was appointed agent in 1864. There also was an agent named R. G. Wheeler, appointed in 1881, and again in 1885, who at one time stirred up some trouble. He wanted to convert the Pima faster than they could take on the new culture and on one occasion they became so threatening that all the women and children were removed from Sacaton to Florence. (See McClintock p. 31), Sun Count, of pure Pima blood, was married to a Maricopa, who died about 1938. One of his daughters married a Navaho. Members of these four generations occupy a cluster of houses at St. John's Mission.

Tashquent is thin, has a splendid profile, and his long hair, which he keeps dyed black, hangs in many fine twists. The old man's hair had last been twisted sixty years before by a native hairdresser who died shortly afterward. The hair had remained in the original strands in spite of frequent shampooing, and he has retained this coiffure because his family is accustomed to seeing his hair worn in that fashion. Stephen Jones described the method of dressing the hair by native hairdressers as follows: Sections of hair were rubbed between the palms of the hands and a stick was used to push the ends into the strands, like braiding. When this was finished, black mud *(bit)* was applied several times to the skeins, which remained rope-like forever. (See Russell, p. 158.)

40

I found Sun Count lying out-of-doors on a bedstead, as he had fallen off his wagon, bruising his shoulders severely. The greasewood treatment had not been used for his bruises, but he had pricked his flesh with hot baling-wire. (Heated nails were also sometimes used.) Although at first I stood two hundred feet away from my informant, I grasped perfectly, by his expressive gestures, the whole story of the accident. Those of the older generation used their hands in talking far more than those of middle-age.

Josie Taylor, who came from Gila, where she lived in a roundhouse, resided at Salt River at the time of my visit. Nearing eighty, she was a poor widow who depended on the distributions of surplus food by the Government. She was a basket-maker, but could not continue this work because she was toothless. Her daughter was living in Phoenix with a negro.

Josie's face was tattooed with a blue horizontal line extending from the outer corner of each eye across the temple to the hair, and with four vertical lines running down the chin from the lips. Cactus thorns were used for the operation, and black gum, charcoal, or *mots* (a mineral which Mr. Halseth says came from the Silver King mine near Superior) was rubbed into the wounds. Mrs. Annie Thomas claimed that the older people used *mots* for tattooing, but the younger generation carried it in little bags to use for paint under the eyes, across the temples, and in stripes down the chin. Isaac Howard said that tattooing was done under the eyes to protect them from the glare of the sun; also for shade, the Pima's heavy bangs were cut low, reaching to the eyebrows. Drs. Castetter and Underhill mention charcoal from a fire of creosote bush being rubbed into fresh tattooing, which left a permanent greenish-blue color. (See Beal, pp. 34-35; Russell, p. 161; Bartlett, II, p. 228.)

During most of my interview with Josie Taylor I would ask her a question through Lewis Manuel, my interpreter; he would then hold forth for several minutes, she would give a grunt which he would relay with a long discourse as if the whole tale had come from her. Some of the information thus obtained follows:

Since eating American food the Pima have forgotten how to cure their own pumpkins, melons, etc. Wheat dumplings, mentioned under *onk ivakhi,* used to keep for weeks, but now they will last only two or three days. Formerly everything was free, and, when cooking was done, it was shared with the neighbors; now, "everyone is mean." Plants, in olden days, were always good, and there was a steady flow of water in the river, but now bad weeds come up because the land is pumped dry.

Indians always had good teeth as they never ate anything hot, but first let the food cool; and they never ate sweets except mesquite.

For snake-bite, the medicine-men would suck the wound and they know how to cure such cases. (See Russell, p. 264.) Josie Taylor has forgotten how to use the native remedies, because the missionaries came and prevented the medicine-men from practicing and teaching, and threw away their feathers and rattles. They also stopped the singing and dancing, and they discouraged the belief in good-luck and bad-luck plants. "We haven't even a rabbit's foot," she complained. "The only way we can learn the right way again, is for the Powers that led us to return and teach and lead us."

Mrs. Annie Thomas lives at Co-op. She is a woman of middle-age, kindly, hospitable, and willing to give information.

Vincent Thomas, at Lehi, lives with and is the stepson of Chapel Thomas who is reputed to be one of two medicine-men still residing in that vicinity. I tried repeatedly to interview Chapel, but did not succeed.

Valensuelo, a Yaqui, lives at Guadalupe, and as I was warned even by the resident storekeeper that I could not possibly procure any information from him, I employed my usual tactics by picking a few weeds, approaching Valensuelo while at work in his garden, and telling him of the medicinal uses of my plants, whereon he responded with an exchange of knowledge. He regretted that Ignacio Luna, a Yaqui living in the same village, had recently died at the age of one hundred and twenty-eight, for he had a wonderful store of knowledge and had been used as an informant; but Valensuelo recommended Feliciana, to whom he sent me.

Feliciana de Vasquez, a Yaqui, was born in Guaymas, Mexico, and was taken to Guadalupe, Arizona, at the age of two. She had a vivid personality, and her colorful costume resembled that of a gypsy. Feliciana was proud of her cures, and more than happy to describe them—in fact, she bubbled over with information and asked me to return soon, an invitation which I should have been only too glad to accept; but after an all-too-short visit, I was forced to say *adios* and we parted with mutual regret—this, after all the predictions that the Yaqui would prove as "silent as the grave!"

Although she was caretaker at the church, Feliciana gave a firm hint that "crossing the palm with silver" would be acceptable by saying, "I am a poor widow, and God alone supports me."

Walkingstick, a bright young Cherokee, is a teacher at Salt River Day School, where Mr. Shannon, the Superintendent, started him on a new project. The children in his class, both Pima and Maricopa, were asked to bring in useful wild plants, which were pressed, mounted, and all obtainable information concerning them noted.

George Webb, a full-blood Pima, member of the Buzzard Clan, fifty-seven years of age in 1941, was born at Gila Crossing and lived there until 1939, when he moved to South Goodyear. He went to Phoenix Indian School and the High School, spoke excellent English, and had the natural manners of a gentleman. He told me that he had conducted some tourists through Sacaton Pass, which winds between imposing pink mountain peaks, and he ventured to explain to them some of his thoughts—that it was a privilege to be allowed to enjoy

43

the beauties of nature. One man answered, "I see no beauty in these d—— rocks," which effectively silenced the Indian.

George had spoken to a negro community on plants used by the Pima, and whenever a meeting of whites and Indians took place in Phoenix he was always selected to represent his people, which he did with intelligence and dignity. On one occasion George accompanied me to the Sacaton Plant Experimental Station, where he indicated specimens of local cactus, making only one mistake in identifying the entire collection. Mr. Peebles was astonished at George's knowledge, saying that he had never met an Indian who knew the cacti so well.

George Webb's own land at Gila Crossing being worthless for cultivation, he moved to his wife's allotment, which is under the irrigation ditch. Here he went into partnership with Mormon cattlemen, growing fodder crops which, if time pressed, he cultivated with a tractor in the moonlight. He handled his father-in-law's property in the same way.

Mrs. Adolph Wilson, a Pima then in her fifties, lived at Stotonic (meaning 'the place of many ants'). She married a Hopi whom she met at the Sherman Institute, Riverside, California, and they lived in an old-fashioned Pima house whose picturesque interior was kept tidy and clean. The door opened into a combination kitchen-diningroom furnished with a range, long table, cupboard, shelves, and a couple of chairs. Two bedrooms were partitioned with corrugated cardboard, matching in color the adobe plaster of the walls.

A few yards away Mrs. Wilson's son-in-law had built an adobe house of three rooms and a screened porch, including a large livingroom completely modern, with several Hopi kachina dolls and a rattle decorating the walls. A framed picture of Miss Hart stood conspicuously on the table, and I noted a washing machine and an ice-chest on the porch.

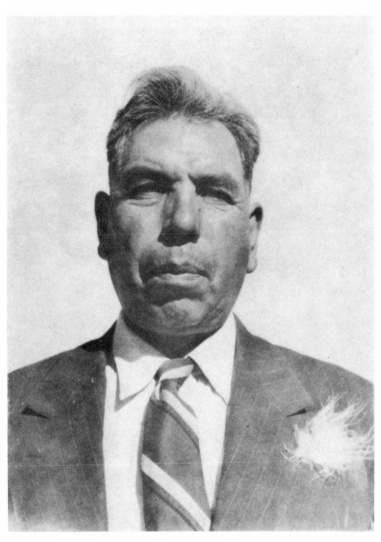

GEORGE WEBB

The plants and their uses
● ● ●

AMARANTHUS PALMERI S. WATS.

Common name: Pigweed
                      Carelessweed
                      Redroot
                      Bledo
                      Quelite
Pima name: *Choohugia*

Family: Amaranthaceae
                Amaranth*

This coarse, *herbaceous* annual, commonly found along roadsides, ditch banks, in river bottoms and irrigated fields, grows so tall and is so abundant that occasionally it is cut for hay. *Amaranth* is a prolific seed-bearer upon which quail, doves, and other birds feed.

Choohugia means 'night carrying.' On the Salt River Reservation the leaves are boiled and eaten with pinole; also, when young and tender, the leaves are cooked for greens and as such are enjoyed by a number of tribes besides the Pima, according to Lewis Manuel.

Lena Meskeer gave me the following recipe as sufficient for one person: The seeds are dried and ground, and one or two handfuls of meal are thrown into a pint of boiling water, a small teaspoon of salt is added, and the whole cooked until done.

● ● ●

AGAVE DESERTI ENGELM.

Common name: Agave   Family: Amaryllidaceae
              Century Plant   Amaryllis
              Mescal
              Maguey
Pima name: *A-ut*

This is a perennial with thick, fleshy basal leaves and a tall stalk that bears greenish buds and pale yellow flowers in June. It is found growing on arid hills, 2,000 to 4,500 feet high. Arizona produces at least eight species, and it is probable that the Indians use several of them; in fact, the Mescalero Apache were named after one of the species from which they prepared an article of food.

A-ut, which is now becoming scarce, grows on the highest mountain in the Estrella Range. After the heavy heart or head is baked in the ground, it is sliced and dried and kept in

---

* NOTE: As this volume is for the layman as well as for the scientist, and since the index is complete, the author has made every effort to simplify the arrangement. Therefore, the plants are arranged under the common *family* name. For instance, the second plant listed is AGAVE DESERTI ENGELM. However, the order is governed by the common *family* name, Amaryllis.

a bag inside the house. The slices may be used at any time and are eaten like candy, stated Annie Thomas.

The leaves are removed from the head of the mescal, which is baked for twenty-four hours in a pit with hot stones. This is covered with more hot stones, a layer of grass, then sealed with earth. Walter Rhodes asserted that the agave becomes tender and sweet, and is served with pinole.

According to Father Antonine, the edible fruit, wet or dry, is called *a-ut*.

(See Castetter, pp. 10-14; Russell, p. 70; Castetter and Underhill, p. 16.)

● ● ●

OROBANCHE LUDOVICIANA NUTT.

Common name: Broomrape   Family: Orobanchaceae
               Cancer-root   Broomrape
Pima name: *Maw-otatk*

My specimen, growing in sandy soil, was collected in the Sacaton Mountains. It is a herbaceous plant, replete with tannin; it has fleshy stems and is parasitic on *Compositae* and even on cactus roots. Kearney and Peebles explain that the name 'cancer-root' was bestowed because of the reputed efficacy of the plants in treating ulcers by applying the stems to the sores. Wooton and Standley tell us that a decoction of broomrape is used by the Navaho in treating sores.

When broomrape first appears in the spring, the tender young sprouts resemble asparagus, and, although bitter, are used in the same manner. They are cooked by covering with hot ashes and baking them in the fireplace; and this is still done by a very few of the old people. The lower part is eaten, but the upper end is discarded, declared George Webb. (See Russell, p. 75.)

CONDALIA LYCIOIDES VAR. CANESCENS (GRAY) TRELEASE

Common name: Lotebush
Pima name: *Oos chuevatpat*

Family Rhamnaceae
Buckthorn

Condalia lycioides is a shrub which grows to a maximum height of eight feet and commonly prefers dry plains and mesas, frequently forming thickets. As the large and numerous thorns keep away intruders from the nests, some people call it "bird refuge," whereas it is known as *bota mota* by the Mexicans.

The Apache use the roots for washing their hair, and at Stotonic also the Pima made suds of the roots for shampoo. At the same place, the thorns were recommended as "a good thing with which to prick," and Catherine Clark elaborated by saying, "To prick the skin over rheumatic pains, after which treatment the blood is washed off with cold water." When collecting a specimen, my informant warned, "Tell her to be careful, because she will hurt herself."

The black berries, which are very sweet when fully ripe, are gathered and eaten raw. A syrup was made by boiling the berries in water; they were then squeezed out by hand and the seeds thrown to the chickens. The sweet juice was allowed to cool and thicken.

Kearney and Peebles state that the Pima treated sore eyes with a decoction of lotebush roots; and Russell (p. 76) mentions that these black berries were eaten.

● ● ●

RUMEX CRISPUS L.

Common name: Dock
                  Curlyleaf
Pima name: *Vakwandam*

Family: Polygonaceae
           Buckwheat

This species of *Rumex,* called curlyleaf, is a naturalized plant from Eurasia; it grows along ditches and sometimes becomes a troublesome weed in alfalfa fields.

Dock leaves are used for greens throughout the reservations. Women at Salt River told me that "the leaves already have vinegar in them and we don't need to add any." At Co-op it is also mixed with other greens.

On the Salt River Reservation, to obtain a yellow dye the roots are pounded and then boiled. Mason McAffee said the yellow edges of ancient Pima cotton blankets were colored by this method.

● ● ●

RUMEX HYMENOSEPALUS TORR.

Common name: Dock
                  Cañaigre
                  Wild Pie Plant
                  Wild Rhubarb
                  Sorrel
Pima name: *Sivijil*

Family: Polygonaceae
           Buckwheat

There are no fewer than fourteen distinct members of the *Rumex* family in Arizona, and wherever they grow, certain species are known to contain a high degree of tannin. The tuber has been used for tanning, dyeing, and curative purposes. This perennial grows in sandy soil, in streambeds, in fields along ditches; it is quite decorative, especially when the seeds are ripened to a coppery red. Even early in spring the large bright-green leaves are very striking in this semi-desert country. Cañaigre is valued among the Pima chiefly for its medicinal properties.

May Makil, whose parents were Maricopa, told me that in olden times the Indians roasted the seeds, ground them on a metate, added water, formed the dough into flat cakes, and baked them in hot ashes. She also said that this same *Rumex* is eaten as pie plant, a recipe for which is given as follows by Miss Elizabeth Hart in her "Pima Cookery": Wash and boil tender red stems, strain off juice, add flour, and cook until thick. Combine solids and sugar with this sauce and fill raw piecrust with mixture; add top crust and bake. In spring, the young succulent leaves are boiled or roasted and eaten as greens, although they are very bitter.

Fat, jolly old José Henry told me that for a cold and a bad cough he chews the root of cañaigre, and when I asked if he swallowed what he chewed, he answered, "Yes, and it stops my cough." The roots are used by the Hopi likewise in treating colds, and are sucked by the Pima for sore throat. Powdered roots are eaten by the Papago for painful throat. At Lehi the tuber is boiled in a little water and when well cooled the decoction is used as a gargle for sore throat, or it is held in the mouth to cure sore gums. For this trouble also, as well as for skin sores, a powder made by drying the sliced roots in the sun and grinding them on the metate, is applied. Should you, emulating the locust of the fable, have sung away the days and not prepared against winter colds, I will pass on a secret that was whispered to me: Oven-baked roots lose none of their potency and the process is speedier. According to Frank Russell, so long ago as forty years, this powder was used in treating sores. Dr. Ruth M. Underhill states that the Papago employ the same method, and I was informed that a decoction of the ground root is used by the Pima as a wash for sores.

In the process of tanning hides, the dry roots are crushed and placed in a vat with water and the leather is soaked therein for a long time. The resultant color, according to May Makil, is a brownish red. To dye willow withes yellow for basket-making, they are left in the liquid for a short time; but if a brownish color is desired, they are soaked for a longer period, according to Ruby Allen. For their yarn, the Navaho obtain a medium-brown dye from cañaigre roots boiled in water; and according to Alfred F. Whiting, the Hopi, because of the scarcity of wild dock used for dyeing, have planted its tubers at the base of Oraibi mesa.

● ● ●

CARNEGIEA GIGANTEA (ENGELM) B. & R.

Common name: Giant cactus   Family: Cactaceae
              Sahuaro or Saguaro   Cactus
              Pitahaya
Pima name: *Haa shan*

This cactus, the largest in the Southwest, bears the Arizona state flower which is pure white and blooms in May and June. Sahuaro grows on well-drained soil and occasionally reaches a height of fifty feet. It has proved to be one of the most useful of all plants to the Pima, and it certainly forms a highly decorative feature of the landscape.

"To keep the stomach warm" and to make the milk flow after childbirth, a gruel is made from sahuaro, according to Fanny Wilson. The ripe fruit is picked with a long forked stick and the skin removed and discarded. A little water is added to the pulp, which is boiled until it becomes light in color; it is then drained and spread to dry. Next the seeds are removed by stirring the pulp around in a basket, then they are ground on a metate and mixed with an equal quantity of whole wheat. Boiling water is now added, and the whole cooked until it resembles a thin porridge, which is seasoned with salt. Lena Innes gave the same recipe, omitting the whole wheat.

The red fruit is picked, split into halves, the skins discarded, and the pulp eaten as dessert. The pulp may also be boiled into a syrup with a little water, the seeds are strained off, and the juice again boiled. The liquid is then sealed in glass jars, and the longer it is kept the more it thickens—like honey. The seeds are dried, and when needed they are roasted and ground on a metate to make a mush, which is moist and sticky, according to Lena Innes. As a substitute for lard, which is used with beans and corn, the ground seeds are either passed through a sieve or left mixed with husks, it was stated by Emma Howard.

The preparation and drinking of an intoxicating beverage (*ha-ashan navait*) made from sahuaro is a religious ceremony of the Papago which, a Pima informant said, they would refuse to describe. When the fruit ripens, it dries, and the wind blows it down; then it is gathered and pressed into a ball five or six inches in diameter, the sugar content making it adhere. These balls are stored in large earthenware ollas, the mouths of which are covered with pieces of cloth tied over the rim and sealed with mud. This conserve is removed as needed and boiled in water to make syrup or wine; in the latter case, it is allowed to ferment for twenty-four hours, then strained. If bottled and sealed, the wine will keep a long time, said George Webb. (See Castetter and Underhill, pp. 20-22.)

Sahuaro seeds, which are known to contain vitamin C, are fed to chickens. According to Miss Elizabeth Hart, a small Indian boy belonging to a poultry club collected sahuaro seeds to feed his chickens. Unable to buy grain, within a few months the lad received first prize for the plumpest poultry with the whitest flesh.

Dead sahuaro ribs, which were used as splints for broken bones, were bound to the injured limb with a rope of human hair, or by twisted cotton, stated Stephen Jones. Mary Manuel advised burning the fractured area with live coals.

According to Russell, sahuaro seeds were used as a medium for tanning, and were available at any time, as they were always kept in storage as an article of food. (See Castetter, pp. 19-20; Russell, pp. 71-72.)

For further uses of the saguaro, see under *Arts and Industries*.

• ● ●

CEREUS GREGGII ENGELM.

Common name: Nightblooming cereus   Family: Cactaceae
                Sweetpotato cactus   Cactus
                Reina-de-la-noche
Pima name: *Ho-ok vaao*

Cereus comes from the Latin, meaning 'waxen' and *ho-ok vaao* means "witches' ladle," whereas the Spanish name, *reina-de-la-noche* ('queen of the night') is far more complimentary. It is a slender, inconspicuous plant that grows at low altitudes and usually among Larrea. Blooming in June and July, its beautiful white flowers last but a night. George Webb told me it could be traced in the dark by its heavy fragrance. Sweetpotato cactus derives this name from the tubers, which ordinarily weigh from five to fifteen pounds. Walter Rhodes stated that the plants are becoming very scarce. Castetter and Underhill write (p. 18) that the large roots are chewed for thirst, or they may be baked whole in ashes, peeled, and eaten.

As a cure for diabetes, Walter Rhodes and George Webb stated that the large tubers are cut up, boiled, and the concoction administered; or the tubers, according to George Webb, are sliced and the juice sucked.

• ● ●

ECHINOCACTUS LECONTEI ENGELM.
ECHINOCACTUS WISLIZENI ENGELM.

Common name: Barrel cactus   Family: Cactaceae
                Viznaga   Cactus
                Visnaga
                Bisnaga
                Niggerhead
Pima name: *Chiavul*

The visnagas belong to the giant cacti of the desert, and, considering their size, have small roots. These two species can be distinguished by their spines. In *E. wislizeni* the central spine is strongly hooked, and there are bristle-like spines on the margin of the aerole. The central spine of *E. lecontei* is usually deflexed or ascending, and seldom hooked, and there are no bristle-like spines. The former species has been known to grow as high as eleven feet and to thrive at an altitude of 4,500 feet. According to Peebles, *E. wislizeni Engelm.* occurs on the Gila Indian Reservation, although the common barrel cactus of that vicinity is *E. lecontei*. Both kinds have been used to make cactus candy.

As I was starting out to collect cacti with George Webb, he revealed to me the following: "When the Indians wanted plants for food or medicine, they went to the hills, and that is where I am taking you first—to the Sacaton Mountains." On reaching our destination, he gave me the method of preparing visnaga for quenching thirst: A sharp stone is employed to remove thorns at the top of the plant; the crown is then scooped out to form a cup; the pulp (which resembles green melon) is pounded, and juice begins to flow. The greenish liquid is neither sweet, sour, nor bitter.

The thorns of *E. lecontei* can be used for phonograph needles, and those of *E. wislizeni* have been made into fishhooks. A sweet dish was prepared by removing the top of the plant and the spines, then the cactus was cut in large slices, which were carried home and cut into small pieces, like potatoes, and, while fresh, were placed on top of dry mesquite beans in a pot with a little water and slowly boiled for a long time. This information was afforded by Sarah Smith and Juana Innes. (See Higgins, p. 64.)

• • •

ECHINOCEREUS ENGELMANNII (PARRY) RÜMPLER

Common name: Bunch Cactus   Family: Cactaceae
               Strawberry Cactus   Cactus
               Hedgehog Cactus
               Torch Cactus
Pima name: *Iisvik*

E. Engelmannii grows about ten inches high in rocky soil; the blossoms are a brilliant rose-purple, averaging three inches in diameter, and are very showy. The spines vary in color from white, yellow, brown, or black. This cactus is found up to 5,000 feet altitude; its flowering season is February to May.

When ripe, the scarlet fruit, which has a network of white spines, is eaten, the spines being removed with a stick. George Webb stated that "the fruit tastes between strawberry and vanilla."

• • •

MAMMILLARIA MICROCARPA ENGELM.

Common name: Fish-hook cactus   Family: Cactaceae
Pima name: *Ban maupai*   Cactus

M. microcarpa is a widespread species that grows in both heavy and well-drained soil and blooms during June and July.

The small red fruit of *ban maupai* (meaning 'like coyote paws') is rubbed on arrowshafts to color them. For earache, the thorns are removed, the cactus is sliced, boiled, and placed warm in the ear. This is also a remedy for suppurating ears. This treatment brought relief to Stephen Jones, the informant.

• • •

OPUNTIA ACANTHOCARPA ENGELM. & BIGEL. VAR. RAMOSA PEEBLES

Common name: Cholla   Family: Cactaceae
Pima name: *Hannam*   Cactus

Var. Ramosa Peebles is a cylindrical-stemmed, bushy plant with strongly armed joints and numerous spines. It bears yellow, red, or variegated flowers which remain open for only a day. The dry, woody joints are made into canes, napkin rings, and other souvenirs for the tourist. If the spines are singed off, cattle, sheep, and goats browse on cholla without danger; and in an unusually dry season I have seen this done on cane cactus in New Mexico. I have also seen Penitentes in that state with cholla bound to their naked backs, on top of which they carried heavy crosses.

About April, using two long sticks, the gemma (buds) are picked before opening. They are gathered in large flat baskets and, to remove the spines, are stirred with a short piece of wood. The bottom and sides of a pit are lined with stones which are heated by a fire of mesquite *(Prosopis velutina)* stumps, as these burns better than any other wood; extra stones are heated to form a top covering for the pit. These and part of the coals are removed and the hot pit is then lined with branches of *chuchk onk* (Suaeda, inkweed), which is also placed between layers of cholla buds to add flavor and to prevent scorching. When full, the pit is covered thickly with inkweed, hot stones, and lastly earth. The contents are allowed to steam or bake overnight and are then spread to dry and stored away. As they make a good balanced meal, the baked buds are ground and made into gruel to be given patients suffering from stomach trouble and needing a special diet, according to Mary Manuel and Catherine Clark.

I saw the young flower buds of this cactus being picked and placed in a flat basket with tongs made of bent mesquite

58

wood. With a twist of the wrist the immature flowers were removed from the plant, and when the basket was full, they were transferred to a large carton placed in the near-by wagon. The buds are taken home and dried, and later are either boiled or are roasted on coals, stated Barbara Harvey.

The dry buds are cooked with *onk ivakhi (Atriplex wrightii)* to flavor the salty greens; they also are ground on a metate, mixed with wheat flour, and boiled to make *atole,* according to Salt River Club Women. Antelope cactus has fewer thorns than ordinary cholla. After boiling the dry buds of this species, they are fried in grease and eaten, or are boiled with meat, I was informed by George Webb.

Castetter (pp. 35-37) mentions the Indians' many uses for Opuntia, as do Castetter and Underhill (p. 14 et seq.) and Russell (p. 71).

● ● ●

OPUNTIA ARBUSCULA ENGELM.

Common name: Pencil cholla   Family: Cactaceae
Pima name: *Vipe noi*   Cactus

O. arbuscula when mature develops into a tree-shaped shrub with heavy trunk and compactly branching crown. It flowers in May and June. The similarity of this species to the cactus that follows, *O. versicolor,* is so marked that I will describe the qualities of both jointly.

● ● ●

OPUNTIA VERSICOLOR ENGELM.

Common name: Deerhorn cactus   Family: Cactaceae
                Staghorn cholla   Cactus
Pima name: *Vipe noi*

This cactus flowers in May and its blossoms vary in color from yellow to terracotta, on the same branch. The yellow flowers wither and turn reddish in the afternoon. The name

59

"versicolor" can probably be attributed to the fact that flowers on *different plants* vary from purple to red or yellow.

The fruit on both Deerhorn and Pencil cholla is always green, and in the spring young fruit ends are gathered, placed in a basket, and thorns removed with a stick. For storage, the fruit is dried, or when green it is boiled with *onk ivakhi* (saltbush) and tastes more sour than *hannam* (cholla). This information was given by George Webb, who conducted me to the wash in Santan Pass to see these cacti growing.

● ● ●

OPUNTIA LEPTOCAULIS DC.

Common name:	Christmas cactus	Family: Cactaceae
Pima name:	*Nafyi*	Cactus

Christmas cactus is found growing from 1,000 to 5,000 feet altitude. It is slender in form, varies in spines, and has very characteristic proliferous fruits, that, is, one grows from the other, forming bright clusters. For this reason it is cultivated in gardens, although my attention was first called to it in Santan Pass.

The coral-colored fruit is gathered in baskets and most of the fine thorns are removed with a brush-like branch. More thorns are rubbed off with a cloth; then the fruit is eaten raw at any time of the year.

● ● ●

OPUNTIA PHAEACANTHA ENGELM.
also O. ENGELMANNII SALM-DYCK

Common name:	Pricklypear	Family: Cactaceae
	Nopal	Cactus
Pima name:	*I - ipai*	

Opuntia phaeacantha is found throughout most of Arizona, growing at an altitude of from 1,200 to 7,500 feet. The blooming season is April to June.

60

Opuntia engelmannii, a bushy plant with stout spines, grows at a somewhat lower altitude and only in the southern part of the state, but it has the same flowering period.

Miss Hart writes that "the tender new-forming leaves are sliced, cooked, and seasoned like string beans." This is a very welcome addition to the diet of desert dwellers.

"If too much pricklypear fruit is eaten, it results in chills and the person shakes all over," stated José Henry; and George Webb explained that there are several varieties of pricklypear—one has light-red fruit which is not poisonous, and another, of darkish-purple, which gives the "shivers."

To encourage the flow of mother's milk, heated pads of the pricklypear are placed on the breasts, according to Mary Manuel.

Mr. Peebles told me that on the Salt River Reservation, Indians are growing an imported Mexican pricklypear for its abundant fruit, and the Mexicans in that locality are so fond of this species that they procure it from the Indians.

The ripe fruit is boiled and white underclothes are dyed in the liquid, said Ida Redbird. The resultant color is a dark pink.

Nopal was applied by the Aztec as poultices to relieve pain and reduce swelling. (See Badianus, p. 243.)

● ● ●

LARREA TRIDENTATA (DC.) COVILLE

Common name:	Creosote Bush	Family:	Zygophyllaceae
	Covillea		Caltrop
	Hediondilla		
	Gobernadora		
	Erroneously called Greasewood		
Pima name:	*Shoegoi*		

This graceful, feathery shrub, covering dry plains and mesas, grows about eleven feet high, has small, strong-scented evergreen leaves, and yellow flowers which bloom profusely in spring. Although the resinous branches make a bright fire, they burn too quickly for practical use except perhaps as kindling. According to Dr. Harold S. Colton, a black gum is produced by lac insects sucking the juices of the creosote bush and forming incrustations of lac over the branches. Lac insects are of great economic importance and have been known to Europeans for more than two hundred years; but the American variety, unlike the Asiatic, is of little use in the production of varnish, although it has possibilities in the manufacture of phonograph records.

Mr. Charles B. Fleming, Jr., of the Botanical Laboratory at Phoenix, informed me that Mexicans pickle the flower buds of the creosote bush and eat them as we eat capers.

To reduce high fever an emetic is prepared by boiling creosote leaves in water, half a cup of the decoction being drunk warm. If the first dose gives no result, a second is administered. For the sores of impetigo, a skin disease often found in children, an infusion is used as a lotion which, I was told, dries up the pustules better and faster than the application of salves. A similar infusion is held in the mouth for toothache, and it was emphatically stated by Jane Pablo that this remedy cures the pain.

On the Salt River Reservation members of the Women's Club call creosote "greasewood," and for removing dandruff they recommend that a warm tea be massaged into the scalp. Two hours later the hair should be shampooed. To prevent feet from perspiring, and as a deodorant, the soles of shoes are lined with small twigs in leaf. Also as a deodorant, a powder of the ground plant is sprinkled in the armpits, and in this form it is dusted over sores. A decoction of creosote gum is given for tuberculosis; and as a gargle and a hot drink for colds, the leaves are brewed into a tea. Branches with green leaves are heated and bound on the seat of pain. The women confidently stated that "this plant cures everything, and that's what nature gave us."

Here are several remedies for the relief of rheumatism: An infusion of covillea is drunk, according to Walter Rhodes.

Valensuelo stated that the smoke of the plant is believed to be beneficial, and twigs are heated and applied to afflicted parts. The Maricopa wear small branches of the plant in their shoes; painful members of the body are held over the steam of creosote, and sometimes a very hot foot-bath is prescribed for the purpose.

At Gila Crossing a handful of the ends of green creosote branches is added to a pint of cold water; this is boiled for twenty minutes, strained, cooled, and taken for gas or headache caused by upset stomach. Ida Redbird suggested that a "handful of greasewood" thrown into a quart of hot water and allowed to boil down, then strained, and a cup of the liquid taken, is efficacious for stomach-ache, cramps, and gas pains. If not relieved within half an hour, another cup was advised for the patient.

Ancient and famous Tashquent recommended "heated greasewood wrapped in a cloth and applied for a bruise," a recommendation that may well be heeded as coming from one of such long experience.

The effervescent Feliciana de Vasquez, a *medica* of repute, prescribed the green tips of *hediondilla* (or *gobernadora*) and mesquite thrown on embers with a pinch of sugar, then the entire body subjected to the smoke as a cure for weakness-laziness. This should be administered on Saturday or Sunday, followed by epsom salts on Wednesday.

Eric Stone claims that the gum is chewed and swallowed by Pima as an antidysenteric; and as an intestinal antispasmodic, a weak concoction of the bark is imbibed. Numerous Papago medicinal prescriptions are listed by Dr. Underhill, as are industrial uses which much resemble those of the Pima.

Professor Maximino Martinez records (p. 133) that leaves of creosote are cooked in water (6 grs to 250) and applied as a plaster for scratches and wounds on the skin. When cooked with 10 grs to one liter of water it is used for baths and rubs for rheumatic pains. The same infusion is taken internally for disuria (difficulty in passing urine).

TRIANTHEMA PORTULACASTRUM L.

Common name None
Spanish name: Verdolagas
Pima name: *Ko okpat*

Family: Aizoaceae
Carpetweed

Verdolagas, locally called "pigweed," as are various other plants, is a common, low-growing, succulent annual found on irrigated land.

On the Salt River Reservation this plant is gathered during the summer, cooked, and served as greens.

I have enjoyed eating it in the spring with a few chile seeds added to give flavor. Also, the Spanish people of New Mexico combine the raw *verdolagas* with salad-dressing.

● ● ●

TYPHA ANGUSTIFOLIA L.

Common name: Cattail
Pima name: *Oodvak*

Family: Typhaceae
Cattail

Like all cattails, those in southern Arizona grow in swamps and marshes. They are tall, narrow-leaved plants, with creeping rootstocks.

Several informants at Salt River School Club stated that the leaves, when green, are woven into mats and roofs; the flower stalk is split and dried for basket-weaving; the silky down makes stuffing for pillows, and Josie Taylor said that the yellow pollen was used dry to decorate face, chest, and back.

In the spring, cattails begin to form buds which contain a yellow powder, or pollen, that must be carefully watched and gathered at the right time, otherwise it blows away. The buds are picked with great care and placed in baskets, and as the pollen is very fine, it must be winnowed into an olla. Mary Manuel, who said, "We go to collect this every day, as we are crazy about this food," gave two recipes for its preparation: A fire is built, and after it has burned down, the ashes are pushed aside; cold water is sprinkled on this cleared spot and a layer of powder spread upon it. The process is repeated until an entire basketful of pollen is used. The top layer is then wet down, the whole covered with hot ashes and allowed to bake until considered done. When removed, it resembles biscuit, and the color has changed to a brownish shade. "You'd swear it contained sugar, but that is its natural sweetness," said Mary. The other method: For every two handfuls of powder, add one of ground wheat, then stir into boiling water to form a gruel. "I use no salt, because I like it sweet," Mary concluded.

According to Tashquent, the tender white stalks and the roots were gathered all the year round and eaten raw.

● ● ●

BACCHARIS SAROTHROIDES A. GRAY

Common name: Broom baccharis   Family: Compositae
            Indian broom   Composite
            Rosinbrush
Pima name: *Shooshk vakch*

Rosinbrush grows in the bottom-lands and on the hillsides up to 4,000 feet altitude, and occasionally is found in saline soil. The blossoming season is from September to March. This shrub is considered poisonous to livestock.

Shooshk vakch means 'wet shoes.' The Pima make brooms from the stalks.

Mr. Fleming, of the Phoenix Botanical Laboratory, told me that Mexicans use the plant for toothache.

● ● ●

CUSCUTA SPP.

Common name: Strangle weed	Family: Cuscutaceae
Golden-thread	Dodder
Love vine	
Pima name: *Vammat geekwa*	

Dodder is a herbaceous, parasitic, leafless and rootless plant, with yellow or orange stems and small, white, waxen flowers.

At Salt River Women's Club it was explained that the Pima name for dodder means 'snake crown' and Indians run away from it because they believe "snake is underneath." On the other hand, Lewis Manuel claimed that "the Pima fear dodder because if a snake sees them take the plant, the snake will get after them."

At Sacaton Flats, cattle feed on strangle weed, although Dean McArthur said they are known to have died from its effects; therefore the Indians fear the plant may be poisonous and do not touch it.

Wooton and Standley (p. 514) state that the Navaho is said to have parched the seeds for food.

● ● ●

ATRIPLEX LENTIFORMIS (TORR.) S. WATS.

Common name: Quailbush	Family: Chenopodiaceae
Quailbrush	Goosefoot
Lenscale	
Saltbush	
White-thistle	
Pima name: *Oedam*	

A. lentiformis, which grows to a height of ten feet, is taller than any other saltbush. It is found in saline soil and is a palatable forage plant.

The leaves are rubbed in water to produce a lather with which clothing and baskets are washed, although it is too

66

strong for the hands. In the past, the tiny seeds were roasted and eaten in time of famine, said Mason McAffee; and we note that they were also of importance during the time of Russell, who gives (p. 78) the following method of preparation: "The seed of this saltbush is cooked in pits which are lined with Suaeda arborescens and the papery inner bark of the cottonwood moistened and mixed together. The roasting requires but one night, then the seeds are taken out, dried, parched, and laid away for future use. When eaten, it is placed in a cup and water added until a thick gruel is produced." He also states (p. 80) that "the root is powdered and applied to sores," but I suspect this knowledge has been forgotten, as I was told that the plant has no medicinal qualities.

● ● ●

ATRIPLEX POLYCARPA (TORR.) S. WATS.

Common name: Cattle-spinach   Family: Chenopodiaceae
           Desert Saltbush   Goosefoot
           Sagebrush
           Allscale
Pima name: *Oedam*

Cattle-spinach, a symmetrical bush often associating with *Larrea* and growing in arid, saline soil at an altitude of 2,500 feet or lower, is well named, as it is an important forage plant. In writing of the Hopi, Whiting (p. 73) tells of the desert saltbush being cooked as greens or added to meat and other vegetables for its salty flavor.

Fanny Wilson remembered that "the ancients," when starving, roasted and ground the collected seeds of desert saltbush to make *pinole,* which tasted salty, whereas José Henry said the seeds were made into bread. At Stotonic the leaves are still used for washing baskets, and Lewis Manuel stated that when *oedam* is not available, *sha-ashkachk eepatkam* ('rough fruit') is used for the same purpose. A specimen was not available.

The white cottony galls produced on this plant by a certain insect are used by both Pima and Maricopa for rheumatism. The galls are gathered and dried. The Maricopa mark the painful spot with a glowing arrowwood stick; a gall is lighted on the cauterized area and allowed to burn; this is done seven times in succession during the same day.

Pima use the above method also in a somewhat less painful way: The galls are set afire and placed on any aching spot either in the muscles or above the bones. This remedy is applied only once, but if favorable results are not obtained, it is again used within three or four days. If a new pain develops in another part, the same treatment is given immediately, according to Ida Redbird.

Mary Manuel described her treatment for rheumatic pains: The flesh is burned by pressing a live coal on afflicted parts and this treatment must be repeated four times "before you can say it's done." Mary explained: "I have a grandson who was the only member of the family who would do everything I asked. My back hurt me so bad recently that I got him to burn it way down low. He was much embarrassed and now I'm afraid he won't ever carry out my orders again." For bad sprains, the same burning method is used. "You cannot feel the pain of the burn because the other pain is so bad. It is only the Maricopa who use the burning, as the Pima consider it too painful."

• • •

ALLENROLFEA OCCIDENTALIS (S. WATS.) KUNTZE

Common name: Iodinebush   Family: Chenopodiaceae
            Burro weed   Goosefoot
            Pickleweed
            Chico
Pima name: *Itan*

Iodinebush is a fleshy, succulent, almost leafless perennial, with a woody base. It grows mainly in saline soil and does not appeal to livestock, although burros will occasionally eat the young branches. For this reason it acquired one of its common names—"burro weed."

When seeds ripened in the summer, they were gathered in a basket and winnowed, then were roasted in a special pot "with ears on the sides," said Sarah Smith and Juana Innes. After this, the seeds were ground on a metate, water was added, and the whole cooked like *atole*.

• • •

ATRIPLEX WRIGHTII S. WATS.

Common name: Saltbush   Family: Chenopodiaceae
Pima name: *Onk ivakhi*   Goosefoot

This *Atriplex* is a tall, coarse annual plant, larger than *A. elegans*. It grows along roadsides and in waste land, spreading over southern Arizona and New Mexico, and into Sonora. Kearney and Peebles aver that this species is held in particular esteem as a potherb by the Indians.

According to Mary Makil, the leaves are boiled in water which is strained off and the greens are then fried in grease. It is salty in taste, as is indicated by the Pima name *onk ivakhi*, meaning 'salty greens.'

• • •

CHENOPODIUM SPP.

Common name: Goosefoot   Family: Chenopodiaceae
           Lamb's quarters   Goosefoot
           Pigweed
           Quelite
Pima name: *Hwahai*

This is a large genus of annual herbs, many members of which help to nourish not only cattle and sheep but also man. Lamb's quarters originated in Europe and are now naturalized almost throughout North America. Kearney and Peebles write: "The Indians use the leaves for greens and the seeds of certain species for making mush and cakes, sometimes mixing them with cornmeal."

Mary Makil related that in spring the leaves are boiled in water, salt added, and when cooked the liquid is strained off; then the greens are fried in grease and eaten. The Yaqui, according to Valensuelo, call lamb's quarters *chichi quelite* and eat them as greens.

• • •

MONOLEPIS NUTTALLIANA (SCHULT.) GREENE

Common name: Indian Spinach   Family: Chenopodiaceae
Pima name: *Opon*   Goosefoot

Monolepis, a small plant belonging to a large family which includes garden and sugar beets, also cultivated spinach, is an annual growing in arid regions.

Gathered while young, during late autumn and winter months, *opon* must be well washed and then boiled in a little water until tender. The liquid is drained off ("juice squeezed out," as José Henry said), the greens are salted, then fried in lard or any other fat.

70

SARCOBATUS VERMICULATUS (HOOK.) TORR.

Common name: Greasewood   Family: Chenopodiaceae
              Chico   Goosefoot
              Chicobush
Pima name: *Schu-goi*

This shrub, which grows in moist saline soil, sometimes reaches a height of eight feet, although it is often lower as a result of browsing. The succulent young leaves and branches attract both cattle and sheep; however, the shorter branchlets are thorn-like and cattle are in danger of bloating by the oxalates in the sap.

Mason McAffee explained that during hard times the seeds were roasted and eaten.

Whiting (p. 74) gives a list of numerous articles fashioned from goosefoot wood by the Hopi.

SUAEDA TORREYANA S. WATS.

Common name: Inkweed   Family: Chenopodiaceae
              Saltbush   Goosefoot
              Seepweed
              Quelite Salado
Pima name: *Chuchk onk*

Suaeda torreyana is a clammy shrub, with inconspicuous flowers and fruit, which grows in saline and alkaline soils and sometimes reaches eight feet in height.

Chuchk onk, meaning 'black salt,' produces flavor in cooking. See *Cholla.*

Dr. Underhill gives the same use for inkweed by the Papago as herein noted for the Pima.

● ● ●

CUCURBITA PEPO L.

Common name: Pumpkin
Pima name: *Haal*

Family: Cucurbitaceae
Gourd

We are speaking here of the cultivated pumpkin which needs no description.

Pumpkin seeds, ground on a metate with a little water added, make a paste which is used to cleanse and soften the skin. In Wetcamp I was told that it is used as a substitute for cold cream.

On the Salt River Reservation the seeds are roasted until brown by shaking them up and down, back and forth, in a pan with live coals. When done, they are cracked with the teeth, the kernels eaten, and the husk discarded.

(See Russell, p. 71; Castetter and Underhill, p. 36.)

● ● ●

LAGENARIA VULGARIS SER.

Common name: Gourd (cultivated)
             Calabash
Pima name: *Vakwa*

Family: Cucurbitaceae
Gourd

Quod supra scriptum est:

Annual herbaceous plants having trailing stems with tendrils; they are related to melons, squashes, pumpkins, and cucumbers. Usage found under Rattles. (See Russell, p. 91.)

● ● ●

TRITICUM SATIVUM L.

Common name: Wheat   Family: Gramineae
                                                Grass
Pima name: *Peelkany*

Although wheat was introduced from Europe, it has lately become the most important crop of the Pima. Harvested wheat is dried in the sun on top of the ramada. When small in quantity, it is beaten out with a long pole *(oos)* of mesquite, willow, or cottonwood; when of greater quantity, the threshing is done with horses.

Stephen Jones of Salt River Reservation told me that in early days wheat was used as money and that a two-pound lard can full was worth ten cents.

Ka poot ka (green wheat in the milk stage) is dried, roasted, and ground, water added, and a "thin soup" made which is given to young mothers to make the milk flow. At Sacaton this gruel is known as *atol,* from the Spanish form *atole,* (Aztec *atolli)* and at Salt River Reservation it is called *koo ul.* Sonora wheat is best for this porridge as well as for *haak chui* (roasted flour), which is prepared by a like method and known to the Mexicans as *pinole,* (Aztec *pinolli*). At Sacaton Flats dry corn is used in the same way, Mary Manuel stating that it is made into a similar gruel to enrich mothers' milk. Walter Rhodes described a thin porridge made from wheat just beyond the milk stage, ground sahuaro seeds, and cholla buds *(hannam),* the whole mixed with water and boiled "for mother's milk." While on the subject of mother's milk, I inquired about childbirth and old Mary explained that in the past, during travail, the woman was made to kneel on the floor or to sit on something folded up and no medicine was given. (See Toor, p. 111.) Upon arrival of the baby, the attendant woman would start pressing on the mother's abdomen to bring down the afterbirth, which, whether male or female, was always buried and

73

the spot covered with ashes. Now, Pima women usually go to the hospital.

Emma Howard gave the following recipe for "poshol" (*pozole*, Aztec *pozolli*): On a windy day, wheat is winnowed in a basket, dampened, and pounded in a mortar with a wooden pestle. The resultant meal is boiled in salted water with cactus-seed "lard" added. Sometimes the "poshol" is cooked with corn, beans, or cabbage. Emma also said that in olden days the women arose early in the morning, ground their baskets full of wheat into meal, added water and salt, and made the dough into tortillas; or they made tortillas and fried them in hot suet, which caused them to puff up. (These are called *wamachida*, meaning 'something made brown' according to Father Antonine.) Often the dough was formed into a single large cake which was buried in hot ashes until thoroughly cooked.

For *matai chuet chimait* ('bread in ashes,' or 'ash-bread'), a stiff dough, like pancake batter, is made of hand-ground wheat, and a little salt added. The dough is formed into a cake, three inches thick in the middle, thinner at the edges. A fire for baking is made of mesquite wood, for this produces the hottest coals, and when it has burned down, the coals are pushed aside and an earthen dish is used to form a shallow bowl-like depression in the hot ashes. The flat loaves are placed in the hollow made by the dish, covered with ashes, topped with hot coals, and allowed to bake for about an hour. The bread is then tested with a stick; if it is found to be thoroughly cooked, it is removed and cleansed of the ashes with water and a corncob. The informant said that the very brown crisp edges taste best. According to Mrs. Adolph Wilson, these ash-cakes are still made and enjoyed as a change from regular bread.

● ● ●

PHRAGMITES COMMUNIS TRIN.

Common name: Reed   Family: Gramineae
                Carrizo   Grass
Pima name: *Vaapk*

Quod supra scriptum est:
A tall, coarse perennial, with flat leaf-blades, which grows in wet ground but is disappearing from the reservations owing to subsoil pumping. Kearney and Peebles (p. 97) give nine uses for this reed, whereas I recorded only two, for making flutes and mats.

● ● ●

SAMBUCUS MEXICANA PRESL.

Common name: Elderberry   Family: Caprifoliaceae
Pima name: *Da hap dum*   Honeysuckle

A beautiful shrub when in full bloom, this species is the only nonmontane found in Arizona. When planted where it receives plenty of water it attains tree proportions. The wood is soft and the stems pithy. Medicinal knowledge of elderberries and their white flowers has spread through the centuries from the Orient, via Europe, to the American continent.

Meta Goodwin informed me that the berries were one of the old foods of the Pima, but that at present they are made into jams and jellies.

At the Salt River Club I was told that, to reduce fever, one-half cup of dried flowers are steeped in hot water which is then drained off and the liquid drunk lukewarm.

The flowers, either fresh or dry, are boiled in water and the decoction is taken, while hot, for stomachache, colds, and sore throat. An old Maricopa used to gather the flowers in season, take them to town, and sell them to Mexicans who used the remedy in the same way as did the Indians. These latter, on visits to Mexico, said Ida Redbird, had learned the medicinal value of the elderberry blossom.

● ● ●

EPHEDRA FASCICULATA A. NELS.

Common name: Brigham-tea   Family: Gnetaceae
             Teamster's-tea   Jointfir
             Mormon-tea
Pima name: *Oo-oosti*
             Koopat

Botanies describe these shrubs, which bloom in the spring, as about three feet high, with opposite stems, slender and jointed; the leaves are reduced to mere scales with clustered inconspicuous flowers and hard, bitter, black seeds.

At Lehi the boiled roots are used as a tea. Tashquent said that the ends of the branches are boiled and made into a beverage.

At Lehi also the roots are dried in the sun, powdered on a flat stone, and sprinkled on all kinds of sores, including those caused by "bad disease." George Webb stated that the powdered roots are applied in this way for syphilis.

Oo-oosti means 'sticks tea,' but I was told that *koopat* is the new name. (See Russell, p. 80; Whiting, p. 63.)

● ● ●

EPHEDRA TRIFURCA TORR.

Common name: Mormon-tea   Family: Gnetaceae
Pima name: *Oo-oosti*   Jointfir
             Koovit nawnov

This species of Mormon-tea, which is the largest in Arizona, sometimes grows as high as fifteen feet and is found in desert or grassland reaching 4,500 feet in altitude.

76

Lewis Manuel asserted that this *Ephedra* is administered as an antileuretic. Other remedies for venereal diseases were related to me by Isaac Howard who advised burnt-bone powder applied dry three times daily to bleeding sores which he claimed are cured in two weeks; and Mary Manuel recommended "burning the boils caused by bad disease with live coals."

Stella Young tells us that *Ephedra viridis* is gathered at any time by the Navaho, and the twigs and leaves boiled with alum produce a light-tan color.

● ● ●

LICHEN

Common name: Lichen on stones
Pima name: *Jievut hiawsik*

As no specimens could be procured, I was unable to obtain the botanical identification of lichen. However, I learned that "earth flower" is the translation of both the Pima and the Papago name.

Mary Manuel introduced the subject by saying: "Men know more about this than I. The Pima men gather *jievut hiawsik* and carry it in their pockets to bring luck in killing game. The Maricopa are too superstitious to do that, for they fear if they carry the plant about too much, it will make them sick."

This lichen, which has a strong odor, is the color of grey ashes and grows on rocks and dead wood in certain spots on the hills. It has more religious meaning than any other plant, and is smoked, mixed with tobacco, at the summer dances, when its distinctive odor is noticeable. Like marihuana, the smoking of *jievut hiawsik* "makes young men crazy." "The Pima believe that if they smoke this lichen they can get any woman they want, but this is just a superstition," explained George Webb.

Isaac Howard described "earth flower" as being "reddish and white and different colors, and smells like violets." He says the lichen is ground into a powder which is not bound on sores or cuts, as it would produce blisters, but is sprinkled on the affected parts. Isaac told of a case where a girl, struck by a rattlesnake, was taken to a hospital and the wound was lanced by a doctor. As it did not heal, she returned home and my informant cured the wound by using the above remedy four times at intervals of several days. Another treatment, related by Mary Manuel, is to apply red coals, when the swelling begins, on wounds caused by snakes, scorpions, and black-widow spiders.

● ● ●

ANEMOPSIS CALIFORNICA (NUTT.) HOOK. & ARN.

Common name: Yerba-mansa   Family: Saururaceae
           Yerba del Manso   Lizardtail
Pima name: *Vavish*

Yerba-mansa has creeping, perennial, aromatic roots which are astringent. At a distance the myriad white bracts give marshland the appearance of a snowy field. The plant thrives in wet, alkaline soil, and my informants claim that it is rapidly disappearing from the reservations because the water-level has been lowered by pumping for irrigation by whites. On my long trips in every direction, the strictest vigil failed to reveal a single specimen. Only one locality where it still grows is known—St. John's Mission at the junction of the Gila and Santa Cruz rivers.

Isaac Howard states that *vavish* is the most useful of all Pima medicinal plants, and he asserts with sincere faith that the wet powdered roots made into a poultice will cure stomach-ache, as it is a slight irritant.

Juanita Manuel says that the best medicine for a cough

is made by boiling the roots of yerba-mansa and drinking the tea, or they may be chewed and swallowed. A prescription for colds is a brew made from the fresh or dry roots, and for preventing a cough caused by an itchy throat, also for sore throat, a dry root is held in the mouth, according to Mary Manuel. For a cold, the hot tea is drunk and the patient is well-covered with blankets to cause sweating. This method is used more by the Papago than by the Pima, states Mrs. Adolph Wilson.

When very tired, Annie Thomas finds relief in a warm bath made from *vavish*.

George Webb asserted that wounds are treated by washing with a decoction of the plant, then a sprinkling of powdered roots, followed by the application of green leaves and a bandage.

For "bad disease" an infusion made from the roots of this plant is applied to the sores and taken internally, stated Mary Manuel. Mrs. Adolph Wilson told me of a Pima woman infected by syphilis, whose first two children died. Her third child, a daughter, was born with "pimples along the groin" and the mother was advised to apply yerba-mansa tea daily. This was done until the rash disappeared; but later it returned and the applications were resumed until a cure was effected. The child is now a grown girl.

● ● ●

MALVA PARVIFLORA L.

Common name: Cheese Weed   Family: Malvaceae
                     Cheeses   Mallow
Pima name: *Tashmahak*

Malva parviflora L. is a native of the Old World, introduced into the Southwest where it is now a common weed. Along ditches and irrigated fields this mallow grows very tall and its leaves are as large as saucers, but the pinkish flowers are rather insignificant.

At a School Club meeting on the Salt River Reservation an old woman told me that she has a friend who boils the plant and makes the decoction into a shampoo.

No uses for the plant were known at Wetcamp, but I was informed that it is called "sunflower" because the leaves follow the sun and droop at sunset.

Apparently Pima children do not eat the green seeds as do white children, who call them cheeses. On the other hand, Pima hogs greatly relish them, according to Catherine Clark. Knowledge of its vitamin content must have been lost through the years, as Russell tells us that the plant was boiled and the liquid mixed with pinole in times of famine.

● ● ●

SPHAERALCEA EMORYI VAR. VARIABILIS (COCKERELL) KEARNEY

Common name: Desert Hollyhock
              Globemallow
Pima name: *Hadamdak*

Family: Malvaceae
        Mallow

When in spring bloom, this and several other species of globemallow are highly decorative along roadsides and in the fields. In *variabilis* the flowers are usually red, although this variety is variable, and lavender or pink petals are often found. The plant, which grows at a maximum altitude of 2,500 feet, belongs to the same family as cotton, okra, and hollyhock.

According to Domingo Blackwater, *hadamdak* means 'sticky,' and *piniendak* 'sore eyes.' Walkingstick explains that this mallow is "covered with hairs" (pubescent) which get on children's hands and then are rubbed into the eyes, causing irritation. "The kids are forbidden to touch this plant," said Juanita Manuel.

I was given three remedies for treatment of diarrhea with mallow: Juanita Manuel stated that a root is boiled in a little water and a tablespoon of the liquid taken in the morning.

According to Fanny Wilson and Mary Jackson, the roots are pounded, boiled, and the decoction given. Barbara Harvey informed me that the roots are boiled in water and the infusion drunk cold.

● ● ●

ASCLEPIAS SUBULATA DECNE.

Common name: Desert Milkweed   Family: Asclepiadaceae
Pima name: Unknown   Milkweed

Botanists claim that this desert milkweed is abundant on dry slopes, mesas, and plains in Mohave, Gila, Maricopa, Pinal, and Yuma counties, Arizona, and that the sap contains an appreciable quantity of rubber. Mr. Peebles mentioned a medicinal plant used by the Pima which is not indigenous to the Sacaton village area, but had been transplanted from the foothills of the Sacaton Mountains to "the Colonel's" garden. I was shown the plant and introduced to its owner, who gave me a graphic description of how Hugh Patton was convinced of its efficacy. Patton had been told that, for stomach disorders, five or six inches of the stem should be chewed and spat out, and that it would prove to be both a physic and an emetic. One day, scoffing at the ancient remedy, he chewed the required amount and started off in his truck; but in a very short time he became convinced that the alleged dual effect of the dose had not been exaggerated.

Edward Jackson could not give me the Pima name for this desert milkweed, and he took me over to see Patton at his store in the hope that he, who is in his seventies, could reveal it, but neither he nor any other informant was of help in this direction.

This plant is considered good for many ailments, including sore eyes. Its use is also very dangerous, as a man below Gila Crossing took too large a dose and in consequence died.

● ● ●

FUNASTRUM HETEROPHYLLUM (ENGELM.) STANDL.

Common name: Milkweed vine
Pima name: *Bann vee-ibam*

Family: Asclepiadaceae
Milkweed

Bann vee-ibam, meaning 'coyote gum,' grows along washes and climbs over bushes and trees.

To make chewing-gum the main stem of this vine was broken and the milk allowed to drip into the green stalk of a squash vine, a section of which had been cut, leaving the joint at the bottom. This stalk was baked under the ashes and the gum was then ready for use. Ida Ridbird said that the Maricopa believed that if this gum were handled too often, it would create boils.

Lena Meskeer still makes chewing-gum by boiling milkweed juice in a deep pottery bowl when pumpkin-stems are not available.

Castetter and Underhill (p. 28) give a list of several gums chewed by the Papago, as also does Russell (p. 78); nor does Whiting (p. 20) neglect to list the Hopi favorite chewing-gums.

● ● ●

PHORADENDRON CALIFORNICUM NUTT.

Common name: Mesquite mistletoe
Pima name: *Hakvut*

Family: Loranthaceae
Mistletoe

Quod supra scriptum est:

A parasitic plant growing from seeds deposited by birds on the branches of trees and shrubs. When mistletoe becomes too abundant it absorbs the vitality of its host and the tree dies. Our variety usually has red berries. Russell (p. 71) states that the berries of this species were the only ones eaten, and Castetter and Underhill inform us (p. 19) that the Papago still gather them for food.

In olden times the medicine-man placed the berries in his mouth, leaned over the patient, and sucked at the afflicted places, then spat out the berries and claimed that he had removed them from the body—an old trick among many Indians. "As long as you believe in anything, no matter what religion you have, you can be cured," said George Webb. Nowadays, at Stotonic, the plant is soaked in warm water and sores are washed with the infusion.

Mistletoe berries were mashed or boiled and, when eaten, "tasted like pudding," according to Annie Thomas. The berries were boiled in water until reduced to a thick mush, which was cooled and a cupful given for stomachache; and it also acted as a purge, on the authority of Dean McArthur.

● ● ●

MACLURA POMIFERA (RAF.) SCHNEIDER

Common name: Osage orange wood   Family: Moraceae
          Bois d'Arc*   Mulberry
Pima name: *S'hoitgam kawli*

S'hoitgam kawli ('thorny fence') is a familiar hedge-plant introduced by whites from its native bottomlands in Kansas, Missouri, Arkansas, Oklahoma, and Texas, where it grows to tree size.

Osage orange is known by its yellow, inedible fruit which is rough-skinned and milky. The inner wood and the large roots are bright-orange in color, and were formerly used for dyeing. (See *Industries.*)

* FOOTNOTE: This was called *bois d' arc* because it was a favorite wood for making bows. "Osage" is from *wazhazhe,* the tribal name of the Osage Indians, corrupted by the French.

• • •

DESCURAINIA SPP.

Common name: Tansy mustard   Family: Cruciferae
Pima name: *Such'iavik*   Mustard

In reference to the crucifers, I quote from Kearney and Peebles as follows: "Few of them have any considerable value as forage, but it happens that species of . . . Descurainia, etc., although avoided while the plants are green, are relished, especially by horses, when the buds are ripe."

Tansy mustard is a desert annual that grows about two feet high, sheltered by any bush, and has yellow flowers resembling mustard. It demands much rain to bring forth a good crop of the minute red-brown seeds, which are shaken into baskets as soon as they are ripe. The seeds are then roasted, mixed with water, and eaten like atole according to information by Josie Taylor.

• • •

SISYMBRIUM IRIO L.

Common name: Wild Mustard   Family: Cruciferae
Pima name: *Shoo uvat*   Mustard

Introduced into this country from Europe, mustard over-runs irrigated districts, producing solid carpets of yellow which enliven the landscapes during winter and early spring.

Domingo Blackwater informed me that ripe mustard seeds were collected and stored for use in winter. When needed they were used for food and also as a laxative, Domingo having eaten them for the latter purpose. Dean McArthur states that a long time ago the seeds were parched, ground, and cold water added to make a gruel. Now, mustard is no longer taken internally but is used externally as a counter-irritant plaster.

For sore eyes, Lucy Howard advised that a few dry seeds be placed under the lids to cause weeping and hence to cure eye trouble. She also suggested that foreign matter can be removed by placing a few seeds in the eye—a far more drastic method than our present-day linseed remedy.

● ● ●

DATURA DISCOLOR BERNH.

Common name:	Jimson weed	Family:	Solanaceae
	Thorn apple		Nightshade
Spanish name:	Toloache*		
Pima name:	*Kodop*		

Datura discolor grows at an altitude of about two thousand feet or under, along roadsides and in waste places. There are other species handsomer and more striking than *discolor,* and I suspect the Indian of not knowing exactly which specific plant is used for each remedy. I merely chanced to show them this variety, and had I indicated *meteloides,* I would have received the same information. It is called "loco weed" by both Maricopa and Pima, and the latter also know it as "poison lily."

One morning at dawn, on a Hopi mesa, I was attracted to a beautiful white flowering *Datura meteloides* which was perfuming the air, but as I approached the plant an Indian woman stopped me by saying, "Do not touch; it is very bad!" This apparent fear seems to bear out Hough's statement in 1898 that "The use of *Datura* is extremely rare and is much decried by the Hopi." However, Whiting, (p. 89) was able to collect several items regarding the plant.

At Fort McDowell Indian Reservation the roots of this plant are used for chest troubles, according to Ollie Goka, an Apache, and the leaves are pounded with salt and placed on sores, stated Mrs. Erilie Jones. They also say that "the plant makes you dizzy." Mrs. Thomas, at Salt River, told me that "if you get the juice from just back of the flower in your

* Footnote: Toloache, from Aztec tolohua, to incline or bow the head; tzin, reverential.

mouth, you go temporarily crazy;" and Mrs. Clark asserted that the "roots are poison."

Mrs. Chaigo said that one must cut the tip of the bud and pour the liquid into sore eyes; and José Henry recommended the same treatment. The buds are gathered early in the morning and, to keep them fresh, they are wrapped in a wet cloth.

According to Mary Manuel, the flower is carefully picked and handled, that the water or dew it contains may not be lost. It must then be heated and placed on an aching ear, although there is danger of resultant deafness if applied too frequently. She said that she "would be afraid to use the remedy, as I am already blind and would just as soon keep my hearing, as now I can at least enjoy talking to people." Old Mary further stated that if a man was hopelessly ill with "bad disease," he had to choose between suicide and the following treatment: He chewed the fresh root of *Datura* and went crazy for a day and a half, and, when he recovered from that, he was cured of his sickness. She thought this malady was unknown to the Indians until the arrival of the Spaniards.

John Scott, of Lehi, said that to draw pus from a boil, a green leaf is rubbed with the thumb and "made slick," then applied; and Roys stated that a certain species of *Datura* was employed to cure hemorrhoids and ulcers. He also gave various other recipes for the use of this plant in treating many ailments.

José Henry related a story of revenge: "A white man settled near a Pima whose horses he killed and fed to his hogs. After stating his case to the American authorities and appealing to them without avail, the Indian dug *Datura* roots and threw them to the hogs which ate them and died." Lewis Manuel had another story: "When the traders first settled on the reservation, they raised pigs, and the Indians got the bright idea of feeding *Datura* roots to the hogs and waiting for them to die. Then the traders would give them away and the Indians would have a feast."

Lewis stated that the small flowering species is the strongest, and when one inch of the root is chewed, "ants look like horses and butterflies like airplanes."

Yaqui women, as well as those of the more northerly tribes, use an infusion of *Datura* leave to mitigate the pains of childbirth. The natives of these areas make a brew from the leaves steeped in mescal to produce a kind of intoxication. For the same purpose, according to Martinez (p. 279), they smoke the leaves and chew the fruit; and also make a salve with the ground leaves and seeds which they mix with lard and rub on the stomach; this mixture likewise produces intoxication and visions. It is understood that all these practices are dangerous.

In the Badianus Manuscript of 1552 mention is made of the medicinal uses of *Daturas* by the Aztec, and many prescriptions are given.

● ● ●

LYCIUM FREMONTII A. GRAY

Common name:	Squawbush	Family:	Solanaceae
	Squawberry		Nightshade
	Desert-thorn		
	Wolfberry		
	Boxthorn		
	Tomatillo		
Pima name:	*Kwavul*		

There are about ten species of *Lycium* in Arizona, where they grow along washes, on dry slopes, or in desert areas, and squawbush bears an abundance of juicy berries. To judge by its numerous common names, the shrub is well known and its fruit has probably brought succor to many drought-haunted wayfarer besides the Indians.

The red berries are boiled and mashed, and the liquid drained off and used as a beverage, I learned from Ida Redbird.

A cup of fresh berries are cooked with half a cup of sugar

and half a cup of water, then flour is added to thicken. Catherine Clark said, "This is very good."

● ● ●

PHYSALIS WRIGHTII GRAY

Common name: Ground cherry   Family: Solanaceae
              Ground tomato   Nightshade
Pima name: *Koekoel viipit*

Ground cherry is an annual herb, the bladdery calyx of which covers the berry, otherwise described as having a fruit enclosed in calyx. It is a member of a large family which includes such useful plants as the potato, tomato, red pepper, and eggplant.

At Stotonic, when asked about this herb, all the women giggled and reluctantly explained that it is not used, but is given the "bad name of old man's testicles."

● ● ●

SOLANUM ELAEAGNIFOLIUM CAV.

Common name: Blue nightshade   Family: Solanaceae
              Bullnettle   Nightshade
              White horsenettle
              Trompillo
Pima name: *Vakwa hai*

Bullnettle is a troublesome long-rooted perennial, difficult to eradicate from irrigated fields. The leaves are silvery and prickly, and the flowers are usually violet, but sometimes blue or white. Kearney and Peebles, (pp. 795-796) state that a protein-digesting enzyme, resembling papain, has recently been discovered in this plant.

Annie Thomas described the following method of making cheese: A pinch of powdered bullnettle berries is tied in a small bag or cloth and placed in an eight-pound lard can of warm milk, to which is added a piece of the dried stomach of a rabbit or of a cow about the size of a silver dollar. After about half an hour the precious bit of stomach is removed, washed, dried, and saved for future cheese-making until it is worn out. The liquid is squeezed from the cheese, which is salted and placed in a cloth on a metate, weighted with a heavy stone, and allowed to harden.

The Maricopa name of bullnettle berries means 'sneeze balls.' Ida Redbird and many other Indians still use the crushed, dry yellow berries for curing colds. When held to the nose they cause violent sneezing. Lena Meskeer said she followed the same prescription with good results.

● ● ●

FOUQUIERIA SPLENDENS ENGELM.

Common name: Ocotillo
Flaming Sword
Candle Flower
Slimwood
Coach-whip
Wolf's Candles
Joseph's Staff

Pima name: *Moelhok*

Family: Fouquieriaceae
Ocotillo

The common English names of ocotillo are successfully descriptive of this spiny shrub with wand-like stems which whip in the wind. Growing on dry mesas and slopes, its bright scarlet flowers decorate the sword-like tips during April and May, giving beauty to the monotone desert landscape. With the rainy season, wedge-like leaves appear which soon drop off and their midribs lengthen and harden into more stiff thorns. The Latin name was given in honor of Dr. Pierre Fouquier of Paris, the term *ocotl* is Aztec, *illo* the Spanish diminutive. Therefore, as pitch pine, *ocote*, was made into torches by the Mexicans, so were the thin dry wands of ocotillo.

When this plant is used green for fences, it often takes root, as one may see in our southern deserts. The Papago used ocotillo for house construction, as well as for many other purposes, while the Pima, as stated by Mason McAffee, planted it to beautify their gardens.

Although Kearney and Peebles, (pp. 583-584) tell us that the Apache relieve fatigue by bathing in a decoction of the roots of ocotillo, and also apply the powdered root to painful swellings, I have found no medicinal properties attributed to the plant by the Pima.

● ● ●

ACACIA GREGGII A. GRAY

Common name: Catclaw   Family: Leguminosae
Pima name: *Oopat*   Pea

The catclaw bears sweet-smelling pink flowers, but has cruel thorns.

Catclaw bushes are cut and allowed to dry for firewood, or are piled high for brush fences; also, we are informed by Lewis Manuel, the wood is employed for making bows.

● ● ●

CERCIDIUM FLORIDUM BENTH.

(This tree has been known under the name C. Torreyanum)
Common name: Paloverde   Family: Leguminosae
             Bigote   Pea
             Jerusalem Thorn
Pima name: *Kuk chue - edak*

Cercidium floridum is a tree that reaches a maximum height of twenty-five feet and grows more abundantly in washes than on plains or hillsides. When covered with yellow blossoms it is highly decorative and most alluring to devotees of color photography. I had only one Pima informant who gave me two uses, although Castetter (p. 38) claims the beans of this tree, ground and mixed with those of the mesquite, were eaten by the Pima in earlier times. *Parkinsonia aculeata* is also called paloverde and is frequently mentioned by Castetter and Underhill.

According to George Webb, the green pods are gathered in summer and eaten raw, and the trunk and larger branches are made into ladles.

● ● ●

KRAMERIA GRAYI ROSE AND PAINTER

Common name:	Ratany	Family: Leguminosae
	White ratany	Pea
	Crimsonbeak	
	Chacate	
Pima name:	*Oeto*	

Quod supra scriptum est:

Sometimes called *chacate,* from Aztec *chacatl,* these straggling perennial herbs grow on dry mesas and plains and are particularly drought-resistant. They are suspected of being root parasites. Kearney and Peebles (p. 421) state that the Papago treat sore eyes with an infusion of the twigs obtained from *K. parvifolia,* and that a dye, used to color wool, leather, and other materials, is made from the roots. From Castetter and Underhill (p. 48) comes the information that a red dye was extracted from the root of *K. glandulosa.*

Oeto roots from the desert hills were boiled and the decoction applied to sores caused by "bad disease." This liquid was also drunk for the same trouble, asserted Mary Manuel.

Lena Meskeer, of the Maricopa Reservation, considers ratany the most important medicinal plant. For sore throat a piece of the root is chewed all day; for fever, half a cup of strong, sour-tasting tea made of the roots, is prescribed. If the pain is not relieved and fever not reduced, the dose should be repeated. For a cough, Domingo Blackwater uses a similar remedy.

Ida Redbird stated that as "an absolute prevention against

infection," the powdered root of ratany is packed down on the navel of a newborn babe after the cord has been cut.

The roots are boiled in water and the liquid makes brown dye, which the informant, John Scott, thinks is used to color willow withes for basket-making. A more detailed description of the process was given by Walter Rhodes: Dry *oeto* roots are ground on a metate and about a pint of the powder is added to a gallon of cold water, which is boiled for an hour. The willows are placed in this brew and boiled for half an hour, after which the shoots are removed, rinsed in cold water, and dried in the sun.

● ● ●

HOFFMANSEGGIA DENSIFLORA BENTH.

Common name:	Hog-potato	Family:	Leguminosae
	Rat's sweet potato		Pea
	Camote-de-raton		
Pima name:	*Iikof*		

Quod supra scritum est:

A low-growing herbaceous perennial, springing from tuberous roots, it thrives in hard alkaline soil, especially when occassionally flooded. It becomes a nuisance along ditches and in cultivated areas. The plant bears yellow flowers, or the stamens are red, and is reputed to be good hog-feed, although the many spherical tubers, about an inch in diameter, are tough.

As described by Lucy Howard, these tubers resemble small sweet potatoes. In olden days they were dug with a sharp stick, but lately with a shovel. When enough are collected, they are boiled and eaten like potatoes and are rather sweet.

• • •

OLNEYA TESOTA A. GRAY

Common name: Ironwood   Family: Leguminosae
              Palo-de-hierro   Pea
Pima name: *Hoi itgam*

Hoi itgam bears very handsome, pea-like flowers, and the leaves are evergreen. I encountered great difficulty in cutting off my herbarium specimen with a hunting knife, as the wood is very tough and the branches are protected by spines. *Palo-de-hierro* has been known to reach thirty-five feet in height, but this is unusual, as the Indians prize its wood highly for firewood, tool handles, etc., and they do not spare the tree long enough for it to reach maturity. My Japanese gardener (confined in a concentration camp) spent weeks polishing a large slab of the trunk which ultimately acquired a handsome glosss, and he made of it a gift that I value.

This tree grows at an altitude of 2,500 feet, also in washes, where the seeds have been carried down. The Pima used to gather the fallen beans and roast them in a pit or in earthen bowls over a fire. The beans were parched and eaten whole, or ground and mixed with water to make pinole, and the flavor resembled that of acorns or peanuts, I was informed by George Webb.

• • •

PROSOPIS VELUTINA WOOT.

Common name: Mesquite   Family: Leguminosae
Aztec name: Mizquitl   Pea
Pima name: *Kwi*

These shrubs or low trees are well known throughout the Southwest and are of economic importance. They bear small, feathery leaves, large straight spines, and yellow sweet-scented flowers followed by bean-pods which are relished by man and beast for their sugar content. The blossoms are a great favorite with bees; the wood is used for fence-posts and as fuel.

The black gum of the mesquite *(kwi choovadak)* has been comforting for many ailments. When boiled with a little water, it is applied to sore lips, to chapped and cracked fingers, as a lotion for "bad disease," and it is taken internally "to cleanse the system." As a tea it is held in the mouth to heal painful gums. Mary Manuel stated that "when the first Indians came, they started using this same resin for sores." Another informant, Annie Thomas, recommended the gum boiled in water and applied to burns, which treatment prevents soreness. At Salt River Reservation, dry mesquite beans are boiled and the decoction used as a bleach after severe sunburn.

Domingo Blackwater asserted that young mesquite roots are made into a tea and drunk to overcome diarrhea.

According to Feliciana de Vasquez: "Mesquite is a cool plant, therefore it should not be given for high fever; but it is good for bad headache and stomach trouble. The green leaves are rubbed between the hands, crushed in water, strained, and a pinch of sugar or salt added. This makes a cooling drink."

My Maricopa informant, Ida Redbird, revealed the following: "To prevent infection in the navel of a newborn child, mesquite gum is pounded into powder and mixed with very fine sand strained through cheesecloth. The compound is then tasted, and if not too bitter, it is sprinkled on the navel and pressed down. For pink eye, Ida's uncle used to pound the green mesquite leaves, boil a handful in water, and place them on his eyes, a treatment that gave him relief."

The Pima are vain about their hair, hence as soon as it commences to turn grey, they resort to a dye made as follows: Mesquite gum is boiled in water and the decoction applied to the hair with a rag. Black clay or mud, which forms in ditches, is plastered on the dyed hair and allowed to remain over night; before sunrise the following morning this is washed off in three tubs of water. "You are uncomfortable during the night, but your hair is very black after the treatment," said

Ruby Allen. The customary shampoo for dark hair is made of *bit,* or black mud, which is plastered on the head, allowed to remain all day, and washed off with cold water in the evening, according to Juan Leonard. Bartlett (vol. II, p. 230) wrote: "They have a singular practice of filling their hair with clay; so that when dried it resembles a great turban. I could not imagine their object in adopting so filthy a custom, unless it was to destroy the vermin."

To make a paint for pottery, according to information by Mary Manuel, mesquite resin is boiled in a small quantity of water.

Lena Meskeer, on the Maricopa Reservation, considers mesquite beans the most important of all wild foods; and Chamberlin wrote in 1849: "We set about to kill some birds but did not succeed very well; however, we should not have suffered, as long as beans were so abundant."

For a good sweet drink, called *vau,* mesquite beans *(vihok,* called *algarroba* by Mexicans) are pounded in a stone mortar, cold water is mixed with the powder, then the product is strained. To prepare dumplings, the beans are boiled in water until soft, allowed to cool, then pressed out with the hands; the remaining liquid is again boiled and small flat wheat-flour tortillas added. This is simmered until no juice remains. On the Salt River Reservation a mush is made from mesquite beans.

From Lewis Manuel came the information that catkins are sucked because they are sweet; and they are called *kwi hiawsik* *(hiawsik,* meaning 'blossom'). Josie Taylor stated that one of the sweets the Indians ate in olden times was mesquite gum which they consumed raw or which they prepared by covering with hot ashes, causing the gum to swell.

See Badianus Manuscript (p. 200); Wooton and Standley (pp. 419-421); Saunders (pp. 61-66); Castetter (pp. 43-45); Chamberlin (p. 179); Kearney and Peebles (p. 420); Russell (pp. 66 et seq.).

• • •

STROMBOCARPA PUBESCENS A. GRAY

Common name: Frémont screwbean   Family: Leguminosae
               Screwpod mesquite   Pea
               Screws
               Tornillo
Pima name: *Koo-ejil*

The screwbean, so called from the character of its spirally twisted seedpods, is a tall shrub or small tree commonly found growing in river valleys, as it loves moist, heavy saline soil. Fresh pods of the bushes are so rich in sugar that children chew them for their sweet taste, and all kinds of grazing animals relish both the pods and the feathery leafage. *Tornillo* is a brother of mesquite, yet it is not found so extensively as the latter. The wood is used for fence-posts and is an excellent fuel.

Roots of the screwbean bush are boiled and the healing tea used for washing sores. Mason McAffee stated that the dry roots are pounded into powder, which is dusted over sores.

To cure a woman who was having trouble with her menses, Lucy Howard gave tea made of the roots of this plant. "She is up and around."

Screwbeans were ground, mixed with water, and drunk as a gruel. This was a sweet and nourishing beverage, asserted Lewis Manuel.

• • •

PLANTAGO FASTIGIATA MORRIS

Common name: Indianwheat   Family: Plantaginaceae
Pima name: *Moomsh*   Plantain

These annual herbs are abundant over dry plains, and hills up to 3,000 feet altitude, and they supply excellent fodder. They bear a great quantity of mucilaginous, shiny brown seeds resembling the imported psyllium.

96

Teresa Conger described the following cure for diarrhea: "Early in the morning, before eating, half a cup of ripe seeds, which have been gathered and stored, and half a cup of water are mixed and allowed to stand a short time. Before this mixture jells too hard, it is administered. The dose for a baby is one tablespoon of seeds to half a glass of water."

This plant requires a wet season to produce seeds, which must be gathered at the right time, for in a few days they become scattered and are gone. White people use these seeds to stimulate bowel activity and to provide lubrication.

● ● ●

XANTHIUM SACCHARATUM WALLR.

Common name: Cocklebur   Family: Compositae
Pima name: *Vaiewa*   Ragweed

This coarse annual gives trouble to both the farmer and his stock, as the burs mat horses' tails and manes, and are dangerous if used as fodder.

M. C. Stevenson states that the poorer Zuñi even ate the seeds of a species of *Xanthium*.

Sacaton Flats Club recommended fresh cocklebur leaves mashed and placed on screw-worm sores in livestock. George Webb says the burs are boiled and a half cup of the strong tea is taken either for constipation or for diarrhea.

Russell (p. 80) was told that the pulp of the cocklebur was combined with soot as a remedy for sore eyes, but its use may have become obsolete within the last forty years, as no one mentioned this treatment to me.

CYPERUS ESCULENTUS L.

Common name: Chufa   Family: Cyperaceae
      Yellow nut-grass   Sedge
Pima name: *Vashai soof*

This and a related species, *C. rotundus L.*, flourish in swamps and are readily distributed by irrigation water. Near Scottsdale the white settlers complained to me that their lawns were invaded by a sedge which they found impossible to eradicate because of the small tubers by which it propagates. Walter Rhodes informed me that the Pima say that the early name for Scottsdale was *vashai*, 'grass'; *soof*, 'scented,' because the plant was so abundant there.

Mr. Rhodes stated that for coughs, or indeed any kind of cold, the fresh or dry tubers, which "pucker like green persimmons and are astringent," were chewed until the taste disappeared, when they were discarded.

Dean McArthur asserted that a certain man at Co-op grew *vashai soof* for snake-bite. A tuber of yellow nut-grass was chewed and the quid immediately applied to the wound, followed by another. When this remedy was used the wound was never lanced, as is done in most cases. In about three days the patient was walking around.

When Lewis Manuel's father, Charles Sampson, who was known as Mooi Choo-edaks (meaning 'has many coals' because of his bad habit of fibbing) went with others to hunt jackrabbits in spring and summer, he spent all day in the chase. To "pep up" his horse, he chewed nut-grass tubers and spat them up the animal's nostrils, according to Lewis Manuel.

● ● ●

CYPERUS FERAX RICH.

Common name: Sedge   Family: Cyperaceae
Pima name: *Vak*   Sedge

This particular sedge is common along streams and ditches up to an altitude of 4,000 feet.

According to Kearney and Peebles (p. 161), E. Palmer reported that in olden times sedge seeds were eaten by Cocopa Indians along the lower Colorado River. At Stotonic I learned that the Pima ate the small tubers which they stated grow on the roots.

● ● ●

EUPHORBIA POLYCARPA BENTH.

Common name: Spurge   Family: Euphorbiaceae
                  Rattlesnake-weed   Spurge
                  Yerba de la golondrina
Pima name: *Vee-ipkam*

This small lacy plant grows close to the ground in sandy soil on gravelly plains and low mesas. When in bloom it becomes an exquisite botanical gem and can be enjoyed even without a magnifying glass.

George Webb described a treatment for snake bite: The wound is lanced immediately, the poison sucked out, and the juice of the spurge plant is squeezed into the cut. The green plant is chewed and the juice swallowed, causing vomiting, followed by sweating. "The man surely is very sick." Angel Sanchez advises that a tourniquet be quickly applied, the wound cut, and bathed with tea made of spurge. A hot poultice of the boiled plant should be bound on before and after retiring, and several times a day. "It will surely cure," he asserted.

Ida Redbird's husband, a Maricopa, boasted that eating

the spurge while driving cattle would not affect him. However, on one occasion he ate too much and was forced to dismount, vomit, and roll around on the ground in great pain. This tale of him was related by his son. Now, when constipated, the same man isolates himself and eats a small quantity of spurge which acts as an emetic and a laxative, but it cures his trouble.

Another Maricopa, Lena Meskeer, chews the root of the spurge, which grows in the hills, for stomach trouble. This makes her vomit and loosens her bowels.

Mr. Peebles told me that this plant, related to the castor bean, is poisonous and that he would rather suffer from rattle-snake bite than take the remedy. While talking recently with an educated Hopi, I brought up the subject of the use of spurge by his people for snake bite and he answered, "Yes, we use poison to fight poison."

Martinez records (p. 300): There exists a hierba de la golondrina *(Muleje B. California)* that appears to be the same species named above, or one closely related. Of this it is said that it has properties of curing bites of scorpions and snakes and is much esteemed for such cases. It is applied locally to the affected part. This has not been proved.

● ● ●

RICINUS COMMUNIS L.

Common name: Castor-bean   Family: Euphorbiaceae
Pima name: *Maamsh*   Spurge

Quod supra scriptum est:

Brought from the Old World tropics and well established on the American continent, this shrub bears large, handsome, shiny leaves tinged with red, and ornamental spring seed-pods. It produces castor and lubricating oil, and is cultivated as a decorative plant. It is poisonous.

When a child, Lewis Manuel said that he would eat the beans without ill effect, whereas the Pima poison gophers by placing several beans in the animals' holes. The dry beans are ground on a metate and the powder is sprinkled on any kind of sores, although no bandage is used.

For constipation and headache two or three beans are shelled and eaten, and they act as a purge, according to Ida Redbird. For the latter ailment, Isaac Howard advises that the brow be bound very tightly. "By this method the pain is made to leave."

● ● ●

APLOPAPPUS HETEROPHYLLUS (GRAY) BLAKE

Common name:	Jimmyweed	Family:	Compositae
	Rayless goldenrod		Sunflower
Pima name:	*Sai oos*		

Jimmyweed, which has a small yellow flower, often grows on overgrazed range land, in saline soil, or along the roadside in irrigated districts.

Juanita Manuel chews the fresh leaves to alleviate coughing. For muscular pain, Fanny Wilson recommended that the skin be scarified with a bit of glass and a handful of rayless goldenrod warmed and pressed against the afflicted part. She also stated that this plant, when dry, is used for kindling, as it burns like paper.

Mr. Fleming informed me that *Aplopappus* is called "jimmyweed" by cowmen because, when eaten by horses or cattle, it gives them the "jimmies." According to Kearney and Peebles (pp. 907-908) the effects are still more serious because if a cow eats the plant in quantity the calf gets "milk sickness" or the "trembles" and the disease is transmissible through the milk to human beings.

● ● ●

ENCELIA FARINOSA A. GRAY

Common name: Brittlebush   Family: Compositae
              Golden Hills   Sunflower
Pima name: *Tohafs*

Two species of *Encelia* are found in Arizona, whereas there is only one in New Mexico, and that is rarely seen. *E. farinosa* is a low, branching plant which, during early spring, covers dry, rocky hillsides with a blanket of golden bloom. The plant is of dome-shape, grows about three feet high, bears gray leaves, and its leafless flower-stalks rise above the bush. The resinous branches make a quick fire and the yellow secretion is gathered and chewed, which was done in Russell's time.

Drs. Castetter and Underhill (pp. 59, 71) state that the Papago smeared this resin on their water-bottles, and to prepare their arrowshafts to receive the points the slit ends were dipped in the boiling gum of the brittlebush. They preferred the latter to mesquite gum, which melts in the sun, and the too sticky secretion of the creosote bush.

Brittlebush spreads into Mexico, where it has been given the names *incienso, hierba del vaso, palo blanco* (white stick), and *hierba ceniza* (herb of ashes).

Mary Beal wrote: "The common name most favored by botanists is *Incienso,* which came to us from Mexico with the early padres, where its resinous gum was burned as incense, exhaling a strong penetrating fragrance. Thence too came the name *Yerba del vaso,* from its use as a pain reliever. The gum was heated and smeared on the body, especially on the chest and on the side. This versatile resin also served as a primitive chewing gum and when melted made a good varnish."

● ● ●

FRANSERIA AMBROSIOIDES CAV.

Common name: False Cocklebur   Family: Compositae
             Bur-sage   Sunflower
Pima name: Unknown

Bur-sage is a common and troublesome weed bordering streams and spreading over irrigated fields. The burs are armed with hook-tipped spines which are difficult to remove from clothing and the coats of animals.

To loosen a cough, the leaves are warmed and spread on the chest and allowed to remain over night. "We warm it up and put it on rheumatic pains, then you get good feelings," said a Papago of the Salt River Reservation.

Angel Sánchez, a Mexican, claims this plant is called *chicura* by the Indians and for women's pains and menstrual hemorrhage the roots are crushed and boiled, as they are better than the leaves. The decoction is strained through a clean cloth, placed out-of-doors over night, and a small cup is administered before breakfast. Sánchez stated that this cures the trouble and that one little root costs twenty-five cents at the drugstore.

● ● ●

HELIANTHUS ANNUUS L.

Common name: Sunflower   Family: Compositae
Pima name: *Hivai*   Sunflower

Sunflowers fringe the roadsides and adjacent fields with their bright golden blossoms. They are tall-growing, coarse annuals with strong-smelling rough leaves and stems. The seeds were eaten by nearly all Indians wherever sunflowers grew, not only raw, but roasted and also ground into meal.

At Salt River Reservation, the inner pulp of the stalk is used as chewing-gum; also, children chew the petals as gum,

103

which stains the mouth yellow. In the same locality the inner pulp of the dry stalk is broken into pieces and strung on a string to make candles which burn down quickly.

Although the taste is very bitter, a decoction of the leaves is made, strained, cooled, and a tablespoon or more is given for high fever until it abates, according to Ruby Allen. Mrs. Goodwin states that the same brew is applied to horses' sores caused by screw-worms. Bringing to mind the question of worms in human beings, I learned from Mary Manuel that in olden days "we did not have them because we ate the right food, but recently my grandchild passed many. All I could do was to make her lie on warm ashes, sprinkle them on her stomach, and massage twice daily. Maybe that cured her, or perhaps she got well because she stopped eating sweetstuff."

Whiting mentions the dried petals of the sunflower which are ground, the powder mixed with yellow cornmeal and used to decorate Hopi women's faces in the Basket Dance. He also gives several other uses for the plant.

● ● ●

PECTIS PAPPOSA HARV. AND GRAY

Common name: Chinchweed   Family: Compositae
                Limoncillo   Sunflower
Pima name: *Oitpa*

This short-stemmed annual belongs to the Fetid marigolds, and its small yellow heads are very strong-smelling. Soon after the rains have fallen, chinchweed carpets sandy and gravelly plains and hills in the Lower Sonoran Zone. My specimen was collected at the foot of Sacaton Mountains.

Oitpa, which serves as a laxative, is picked in the flowering season as at that time it contains the medicinal property. The fresh plant is boiled in water, allowed to steep, and strained off; or the dry plant is prepared in the same way and makes a stronger tea. George Webb said that this decoction can be drunk in large quantities throughout the day.

104

• • •

PLUCHEA SERICEA (NUTT.) COVILLE
(BERTHELOTIA SERICEA RYDB.)

Common name: Marsh-fleabane   Family: Compositae
      Arrow-wood   Sunflower
      Arrow-weed
      Cachanilla
Pima name: *Oos hawkmaki*

Flowering in the spring, this rank-smelling shrub forms dense thickets along streams throughout the state in the Lower Sonoran Zone. It is browsed by deer, horses, and cattle, and the pinkish flowers are an important source of honey.

A medicine-man could effect an immediate cure for snake bite on a horse by chewing the roots of arrow-weed and spitting on the open sore, according to Isaac Howard. Stephen Jones said that a tea made of the roots boiled in water is good for sore eyes.

For stomachache and diarrhea, the roots are washed, crushed while still fresh, and boiled into a strong tea, a cup or two of which is administered. Ida Redbird has tested this remedy with success. She also suggests chewing the root and applying it all over the body to sooth a nervous child that cries out in its sleep.

In olden days a fire was started by twisting a length of dry arrow-wood between the palms of the hands with a downward movement into a groove made in a sahuaro rib. Dry horse manure was used as tinder. In pottery-making any wood was used for the bed of coals, and the kiln was built of cow manure, I was informed by Stephen Jones.

• • •

SONCHUS OLERACEUS L.

Common name: Sowthistle   Family: Compositae
Pima name: *Hwai hoehoevo*   Sunflower

Quod supra scriptum est:

A coarse, succulent annual introduced from Europe and now common along roadsides and in waste places. Kearney and Peebles (p. 1028) give the following information: "A gum obtained by the evaporation of the juice of this plant is said to be a powerful cathartic and it has been used as a so-called cure for the opium habit."

Hwai hoehoevo ('deer lashes') tastes sweet, and the leaves are rubbed between the palms of the hands and eaten raw, as are the ender stems. The leaves are also cooked as greens, stated Lewis Manuel. When they are young and tender, these greens are boiled in salted water, with chile added, and eaten by the Yaqui, I was informed by Valensuelo.

• • •

SONCHUS ASPER (L.) HILL

Common name: Sowthistle   Family: Compositae
Pima name: *S'hoitgamivakhi*   Chicory tribe
                                                 Sunflower

Sonchus asper, naturalized from Europe, is found in six Arizona counties and is a common weed in gardens and cultivated fields.

'Prickly greens' was the meaning given by Women's Club for *s'hoitgamivakhi.* The tender leaves are rubbed between the palms and eaten raw, or they are cooked as greens. The stalks are peeled and eaten raw like celery, said Walkingstick, and according to Lewis Manuel these stems quench thirst and the whole plant is bitter.

Russell (p. 77) says that "the leaf of this thorny plant is eaten raw or boiled."

106

● ● ●

TAMARIX APHYLLA

Common name: Tamarix
                  Salt cedar
Pima name: *Svockhi oos*

Family: Tamaricaceae
           Tamarix

Tamarix, naturalized from North Africa, is a large shrub or tree cultivated for hedges. A handsome, feathery plant, it bears minute flowers varying in shade from white to dark pink.

Svockhi oos ('red stick') is planted for winter wood supply and for its grateful shade which keeps summer kitchens cool, although the Indians complain that nothing else will grow within a large radius of the trees.

● ● ●

MARTYNIA PARVIFLORA WOOTON
MARTYNIA ARENARIA ENGELM.

Common name: Devilsclaw
                  Unicornplant
                  Devilhorns
Pima name: *Ihuk*

Family: Martyniaceae
           Unicornplant

Martynias are coarse, clammy, annual herbs with thick stems, sizable leaves, and few flowers. They bear large, fleshy, beaked pods which, when dry, split into hooklike appendages. *Ihuk* is cultivated by the Pima for use in basket-making, although it grows wild on plains and mesas.

Two species of *Martynia* occur on the reservation, *M. parviflora Wooton* and *M. arenaria Engelm.* The former, according to information from local Indians, is the species most used in basketry. It has comparatively small purple flowers, while *M. arenaria* has larger, yellow flowers. The young pods are used for food by natives in Sonora, and the Papago still use them for this purpose. Mr. Odd Halseth stated that the dry

107

seeds are cracked between the teeth and eaten like pine-nuts by the Pima.

For rheumatic pains a small piece of claw is broken off and pressed into the flesh, then lighted and allowed to burn. "Just for fun" the fresh seeds are chewed and the juice swallowed according to George Webb.

● ● ●

SALIX GOODDINGII BALL

Common name: Willow   Family: Salicaceae
Pima name: *Chi ul*   Willow

These trees, which grow to the height of forty-five feet, are to be found along streams throughout most of Arizona.

Eric Stone (p. 35) states that the Pima and other tribes made a decoction of the leaves and bark which they drank as a febrifuge. The efficacy of this remedy is further verified by Kearney and Peebles (pp. 216-217), who tell us that the drug salicin, obtained from the bark of various willow species, has febrifugal value, as well as other properties. (See *Industries.*)

The Pima distinguish between the full-grown tree and the young shrub-like shoots, insisting that they are different species. *Chi ul* signifies "sweet," and the catkins are eaten raw.

In making the outdoor storage basket, *hawmda,* the work is commenced with wands from this willow. Slips are planted to form fences, Lewis Manuel stated.

● ● ●

POPULUS FREMONTII S. WATS.

Common name: Valley cottonwood Family: Salicaceae
Pima name: *Aupa (Aupa haupuldak)* Willow

A great boon to the arid Southwest is the cottonwood tree, often planted for its refreshing shade. Preferring broad river valleys where the soil is moderately moist, occasionally it reaches 100 feet in height and a circumference of four feet. The buds are resinous, the catkins long and drooping, and the wood is light and pulpy.

Fence-posts are made of cottonwood, which is useful also as fuel, but it is poor in either case. The young green pods, *aupa haupuldak,* are chewed as gum and the twigs are employed in certain basket-making at Lehi.

A handful of *aupa ha hak* (cottonwood leaves) is boiled in a pint of water and sores are washed with the decoction. Like greasewood, this is very healing. For hair-dye a brew was made from cottonwood leaves, strained and mixed with tea from mesquite bark on the Salt River Reservation.

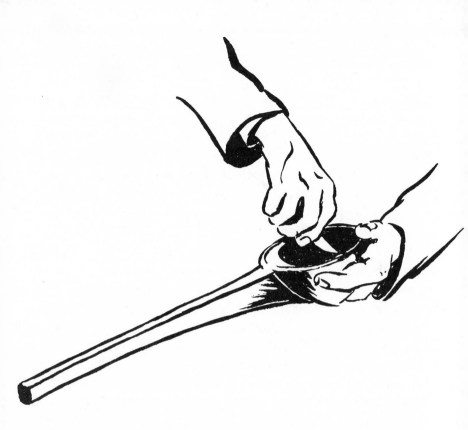

Art & Industries
• • •

HOUSE BUILDING

Informant: Mason McAffee

Nine forked mesquite *(kivi)* posts, green or dry, are sunk two feet in the ground, with about seven feet above ground and five or six feet apart according to the length of the three main cross-beams, which are usually of cottonwood, but never of mesquite, because it does not grow straight. The ends of the cross-beams are placed in the forks of the uprights. Transverse beams of cottonwood *(aupa)* or willow *(chi ul)* are laid about one foot apart over the main beams. Arrowwood *(oos hawkmaki)* stems are next laid close together across the lesser beams to form the ceiling; to make the eaves these are extended about a foot beyond the walls. When plentiful, cattails are employed for this purpose, as they make a neater finish. After harvest, wheat straw is laid across the arrowwood. For finishing the roof mud is tramped down and sloped downward toward the eaves. In olden days any kind of mud was used; but now the Indians prefer the clay on banks of irrigation ditches. Women carried the mud in baskets; in modern times a wagon is used.

For the walls, small willow poles are stuck into the ground, about two feet apart, and bound to the upper poles with green willow shoots or bark. Willow or slender cottonwood poles are tied horizontally across the uprights about two feet apart, then arrowweed is stood up close together and held in place with crossbars outside, which are tied on. Nowadays entire houses are often bound together with baling-wire. Walls are plastered both inside and out. According to Mrs. Emma Howard, dry ribs of dead sahuaro are collected and used to form the framework of a house. Floors are covered with sand to prevent dust from rising; but in summer they are kept sprinkled, which helps to maintain a comfortable temperature. There are neither windows nor chimneys, the only opening being the entrance. In the past, doors, as well as sleeping mats, were made of *vaapk,* which my informant translated as 'bamboo,' but doubtless it was a cane that no longer grows in the river-bottoms. (See Russell, p. 147.)

An important adjunct to a Pima dwelling is the ramada (Spanish, *enramada*), or arbor *(vahto),* which is constructed in the same manner as the framework for the house. In order to obtain the best circulation of air, it is built a short distance away from the dwelling. In the shade of the ramada in summer the Pima spend most of their waking and sleeping hours. When there is no outside kitchen, cooking is done here and

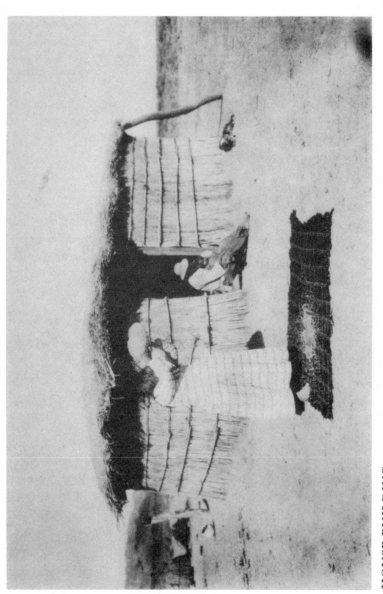

HOUSE BUILDING

HOUSE BUILDING

the food is served on a table therein. Bedsteads are also installed.

When a youth married, he took his bride to his father's house, and not until that house became over-populated did he build himself one with the help of his friends.

● ● ●

ROUND HOUSES

Round houses have become obsolete; indeed I saw only one —that of José Henry on the Salt River Reservation, but this, I presume, was a poor example, having degenerated from the original type; therefore I deem it best to use the descriptions given by former observers, which more or less accurately picture old José's hut. Emory (p. 85) described a round house as follows:

"I rode leisurely in the rear, through the thatched huts of the 'Pimos'; each abode consists of a dome-shaped wicker work, about six feet high, and from twenty to fifty feet in diameter, thatched with straw or corn stalks. In front is usually a large arbor, on top of which is piled the cotton in the pod, for drying."

In 1850-53, Bartlett, (vol. II, pp. 233-234) observed the dwellings of the "Pimo" Indians, and in 1901-02 Russell (p. 154, pl. XXXV) gave a more detailed account of the construction of the round house which I quote:

"The central supporting framework is usually entirely of cottonwood though other timber is sometimes used. The lighter framework is of willow, on which is laid the arrowwood, cattail reeds, wheat straw, cornstalks, or similar material that supports the outer layer of earth.

"The roof is supported by four crotched posts set in the ground 3 or 4 m. apart, with two heavy beams in the crotches. Lighter cross poles are laid on the last, completing the central framework. Light willow poles are set half a meter in the ground around the periphery of the circle, their tops are bent in to lap over the central roof poles, and horizontal stays are lashed to them with willow bark. The frame is then ready for the covering of brush or straw. Although earth is heaped upon the roof to a depth of 15 or 20 cm. it does not render it entirely waterproof. When finished the *ki* is very strong and capable of withstanding heavy gales or supporting the weight of the people who may gather on the roof during festivals."

● ● ●

SHELVES

Informant: George Webb

The thorns of the ocotillo *(moelhok)* were removed, the stalks bound together with rawhide or wire, and suspended from the ceiling as shelves. Dry sahuaro ribs were used for the same purpose.

● ● ●

BOWS

(Oos gaat, meaning 'wooden guns')
Informant: Vincent Thomas

Hunting bows of the Pima are rather crude and are not decorated. Osage orange wood is preferred, but they are also made of willow *(chi ul),* and of catclaw *(oopat)* from the mountains. The trunk of a young osage orange tree about twelve inches in circumference is cut down and while green is split into halves and then shaped to the desired size with a butcher knife. The bow is bent to the proper arc and fastened with wire until thoroughly dry.

Another method was followed by Lewis Manuel, who also used osage orange wood, but while the bow is green it is bent between the forked branches of a tree and allowed to dry in that position. For decoration, ochre *(hoe-et)* and black earth *(mots),* which are dug in the mountains, are used; and soot from pots is also sometimes employed.

Jumbi Juan's bow, made of osage orange, was nearly five feet long. His bowstring *(giadak)* was made of twisted horse-sinew, but the mice had gnawed it. Bow-guards were made of rawhide, although for a well-rounded bow they were not necessary.

Before the introduction of domestic animals, deer supplied the sinew for making bowstrings, but now the sinew is taken from the back of a dead horse or cow. The sinew is dried, then soaked, stretched, and the strands twisted together into a two-ply cord which is attached to a notch cut within an inch or so of each end of the bow. (See Russell, p. 95.)

● ● ●

ARROWS
Informant: Vincent Thomas

Arrows *(hapot;* plural, *haapot)* are made from straight arrowwood shafts which are pointed at one end, and having either two or three chicken or hawk feathers attached to the other sinew. Another informant, Lewis Manuel, stated that sinew is wrapped near the point of an arrow to keep it from splitting.

Castetter and Underhill (p. 72) state that both arrow-bush and creosote-bush were used for arrowshafts.

● ● ●

CARRYING BASKETS
Pima name: *Gioho*
Informant: Mrs. Adolph Wilson

When Mrs. Wilson was a very small child her grandmother used to carry her and firewood together in a burden basket which was made as follows:

Twisted agave fiber was acquired from the Papago and woven into a truncated cone of the desired size, the upper circumference of which was braced by a strong willow hoop. A design was woven in and afterward intensified by black and red colors. Two long saguaro poles were tied together near the bottom and placed in front, and two short ribs of saguaro were fastened at the rear, which fiitted against the back. The willow hoop was attached to the four sticks by a cord of human hair, and the wrapping was continued around the ends of the poles.

A matting headband and an apron to protect the back were obtained from the Papago. The headband was attached to the willow hoop with a hair rope. The informant said that she remembers strands of her hair being cut frequently for this purpose.

An extra helping stick, forked at the top, was used in conjunction with the two long ribs to form a tripod which braced the basket for loading and also helped the bearer to rise. Looking toward the opening, the burden basket is round, and conical in side view. Sizes vary with that of the bearer. (See Russell, pp. 140-143, pl. 34; Mason, fig. 100, p. 295.)

● ● ●

COILED BASKETS FOR HOUSEHOLD USE

Informant: Teresa Conger

Pima basketry has intricate and striking designs, and the stitches are fine and the finish smooth. Small branches of *Salix Gooddingii (chi ul)* are collected and split in two when green, immediately peeled, twisted in a circle, and allowed to dry in the sun. The sewing is done with these withes. Seedpods of the unicorn plant, *Martynia parviflora (ihuk)*, are used for the black designs. These plants grow voluntarily in the cornfields, but if not sufficient in quantity, they are cultivated. The dry pods must be soaked and split from their points downward;

116

the ends are cut off and the splints are buried in wet earth to keep them pliable while the work is in progress. These black strands are twelve inches or longer, and so tough that they outwear the willow.

Cattail stalks, Typha *(oodeak)*, are gathered in August and when green are peeled and split into halves, then laid on the ground to dry and bleach in the sun; next they are split very thin, dampened, and twisted with the black strands to start the center of the basket. The end of the split cattail is held between the teeth while the work continues. The distance for the design is measured while the stitching proceeds, and the ends of both types of withes are carefully hidden. The margin of the basket is finished by braiding either material in and out.

Implements used in basketmaking are a knife to cut the white and black strands according to design, and an awl to make the stitches. (See Russell, p. 135; Castetter and Underhill, pp. 56-59; Mason, figs. 198 to 203, p. 519.)

● ● ●

INDOOR STORAGE BASKETS

Informant: Emma Howard

The storage basket for indoors, called *vashom,* is not so coarse as that which is made to keep out-of-doors. Wheat straw is cut as long as possible, and dampened slightly to make it flexible. The bottom of the basket is formed by coiling this straw, which is then stitched tightly together with soaked, young mesquite *(kwi)* bark. A large awl or needle made of hardwood, which through long service becomes polished, is used to pierce a hole through the straw. The basket bottom is about two feet in diameter and as the basket is built up it is widened to about four feet, but gradually becomes narrower at the top which must be sufficiently large to admit a person, as the arm is not long enough to reach the grain as it is used. When the basket is full of wheat, the cover is put into place and sealed with a paste made of strongly alkaline earth, which is salty and keeps away mice. The Pima kept these baskets in their storehouses, and in olden days, when the children were first required to attend school, mothers would hide their little ones in these large receptacles. Once a small girl was discovered and carried off by the authorities because of her outcry when stung by a scorpion.

In connection with the above, Lewis Manuel stated that storage baskets were unsealed and the basektry covers removed when the roadrunner (*d'adai*) first sang in the summer; but now no attention is paid to the old laws, and his wife will open the cans of corn which she has put up, whenever she likes. (See Bartlett, vol. II, p. 235; Mason, p. 524.)

● ● ●

OUTDOOR STORAGE BASKETS

Informant: Stella Conger

To make a storage basket (*hom ta*): Green wands of arrowwood or sweet willow are twisted into a four-foot circle and bound with wire. The sides are then built up with green arrowwood branches, the leaves left on. The large ends are stuck into the lower circle to anchor them, and the brush is twisted into rolls and coiled, gradually narrowing until the top of the basket is reached. The depth of the basket is about two feet. A platform is made of two layers of crossed logs on which strips of thick arrowwood branches are laid close together and the basket is placed thereon. The bottom of the receptacle is lined with straw and a bag of wheat is stored within to keep safely through the season. The basket is then covered with arrowwood branches and earth. It requires about two days' work to build this basket receptacle.

CARRYING BASKETS

CRADLES

● ● ●

BIRD-CAGES

Informant: Lewis Manuel

Bird-cages were made from willow withes *(chi ul)* or from arrowwood and were tied with strips of willow-bark. These cages confined eagles, doves, and hawks for the great hunters who used their feathers for arrows. (See Russell, p. 102.)

● ● ●

CRADLES

Pima name: *Woolkut*

Informants: George Webb and Lewis Nelson

A frame was constructed of green screwbean or catclaw branches, or of mesquite root. The latter were approximately four feet long and about half an inch or an inch in circumference. The material was bent in an elongate "U," with the sides about eight inches apart, and in this form it was allowed to dry. Dead sahuaro ribs were sometimes used as cross-pieces, also cottonwood or mesquite sticks which had been flattened by being split, and they were left a trifle longer than the width of the frame. These slats were notched an inch or so from each end and bound on the frame with sinew two or three inches apart, running three-fourths of the way down the cradle. In some cases this structure was padded all around and bound with strips of willow-bark to keep the baby in and to make it more comfortable. The bark padding on the curved head-piece was higher than the sides. Stripped inner bark of cottonwood or dead willow was stretched the length of the cradle and hung down beyond the last cross-bar. Over this soft and absorbent layer, a thrice-folded, hand-woven cotton blanket was arranged. The baby was placed on the blanket and its head lay in a soft depression instead of on a hard board, as was frequently the case in other tribes. The position of the baby

119

was often changed to prevent flattening of the back of the skull. A small, light, cotton blanket covered the infant, being bound to the cradle with homespun and hand-woven cotton tape four or five feet long and about four inches in width. At a later period, for weaving these tapes, the parents bought aniline-dyed Germantown wool when they could afford it, which was woven into various designs.

A detachable hood was made by weaving strips of willow-bark in and out of twenty or more willow withes. These withes were first bound closely together at the end, leaving the hood wide at the top and gradually decreasing to a few inches on the underside. The weaving was done in patterns which, for decoration, were accentuated by the use of colors.

● ● ●

LADLES

Informant: Pelvin Newman

Ladles made of mesquite wood are to be found in every house. Pelvin Newman makes them from the trunk of a mesquite, which will produce from four to six ladles. The wood must be worked while green, as it is very hard and will crack when dry. Newman starts by splitting the trunk with a small hatchet, which he also uses for the first rough shaping; then he employs a steel gouge which he pounds with a wooden mallet, smoothing and finishing the ladle with a butcher knife. No drawing is made for a pattern. The wood is dampened from time to time as the work progresses. Newman makes mixing bowls of the old-fashioned kind, and for modern trade he also manufactures rough rolling pins. It requires four days to make four ladles, for which the Indians pay him a dollar apiece. When Newman was young, he made bows out of willow, but there is no demand for them now. (See Russell, p. 101, figs. 14b, 14c.)

According to George Webb, the trunk and larger branches of paloverde are also made into ladles.

● ● ●

MORTARS

Pima name: *Chuepa*
Informant: Stephen Jones

While gathering material from Stephen Jones, I spied a mortar made of cottonwood, measuring about three feet across and having very thick walls. The log lay horizontal with a circular hole cut out of the side. A large stone pestle *(veetkut)* was used in crushing mesquite beans in the mortar. I asked to have this mortar, now a rare household utensil, deposited in the museum for safekeeping, but was told that it was constantly in use, although I had found it under a discarded baby's crib in the front yard. The hole was completely filled with chicken droppings. (See Russell, p. 99, figs. 13a, 13b.)

● ● ●

SHOVELS

Informant: Stephen Jones

The informant had heard of shovels made of ironwood and cottonwood, but had never seen one. In his youth the Pima used small shovels made from iron they had found and taken to a blacksmith in Tucson, who fashioned it into tools. (See Russell, p. 97, fig. 10b.)

● ● ●

ROPE

Informants: George Webb, Stephen Jones, and Lewis Manuel

Long ago the dead leaves of agave *(a-ut)* were cut with a sharp stone, beaten with another stone, the fibers straightened out, split, and then rolled into a great ball. It required two men to twine the fiber into a cord, several of which were in turn twisted into a rope by tying them to the end of a rope-twister. This implement was made of two mesquite sticks, the longer one having a hole in one end, through which the shorter stick was thrust to serve as a handle, which was prevented from slipping off by a forked end or a carved button, but was free to turn. Then the rope-twister was whirled. In this manner, also, rope was made from human hair, and later from horsehair. The latter was in different colors: black, white, and red. (See Russell, pp. 106, 114, figs. 23, 37.)

● ● ●

BROOMS

Informant: Mrs. Fulwiler

Any time of the year, stalks of Indian broom *(shooshk vakch)* are cut about four feet long and tied together at one end with a string. This broom is used green for sweeping the yard, because when dry it becomes too brittle and has to be discarded.

● ● ●

FLUTES

Informant: George Webb

Formerly flutes were ceremonial instruments, but now they are fabricated solely for the music they can be made to produce. The method is as follows: The cane is cut, leaving two entire sections and about an inch protruding beyond the two end nodes, which are pierced by burning or drilling. Then a hole is pierced on each side of the center joint, and a groove made between them. Three holes are drilled for the fingers, and a ribbon is tied over the upper part of the groove to force the air down.

Bartlett (vol. II, p. 222) in 1850-53 described the use of the flute in courtship: "The fair one's attention is sought . . . To do this, he takes his flute, an instrument of cane with four holes, and, seating himself beneath a bush near her dwelling, keeps up a plaintive noise for hours together. This music is continued day after day; and if no notice is at length taken of him by the girl, he may 'hang up his flute,' as it is tantamount to a rejection."

● ● ●

DRUMS

Informant: Lewis Manuel

The only drum the Pima had was an inverted basket on which they beat with two sticks.

● ● ●

RATTLES

Informants: Lewis Manuel and Jumbi Juan

Before the white man came, cultivated gourds, or calabashes, served as rattles, canteens, and dippers, but now they are used principally for rattles. Jumbi Juan fashioned the latter in the following manner: The gourd was dried, a hole pierced in the top and the bottom, the seeds removed, and the inside filled with enough gravel from ant-hills to produce a satisfactory sound. A stick of mesquite-root was thrust through both holes and tightly fitted. For decoration, holes were bored with an awl in any design that pleased the maker, and burning charcoal was used for coloring. Lewis Manuel had on hand a gourd of the proper size for making into a rattle for accompanying his sacred Pima ceremonial songs, although after his marriage he voluntarily joined the Mormon faith. He told me that he knows of no further use for the wild gourd *(adam)*.

Games

• • •

GAMBLING GAME "GINS"

Informant: Lewis Manuel

In this game a court was provided, consisting of a level space, nine by thirteen feet, the southwest corner of which is called the "house" *(kee)*, where ten holes are scooped out of the ground. The other three corners have only nine holes. The implements used are four sticks (about 6¾ inches by ¾ of an inch), originally made of arrowwood, which grew large when water was plentiful, but now are made of mesquite root and so split that they have a rounded and a flat side. These

125

Sample of "horses" used

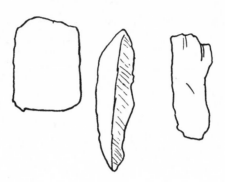

The flat sides of sticks are marked and named as below:

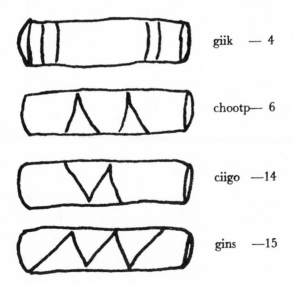

giik — 4

chootp— 6

ciigo —14

gins —15

THE GAME OF GINS

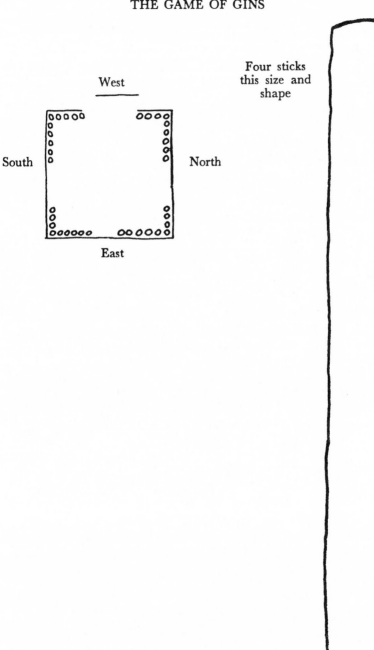

West

South

North

East

Four sticks
this size and
shape

sticks have various markings which indicate their numerical values, and the counting is very complicated. A flat stone is employed to hit the bottom ends of the sticks which are held loosely at a slight angle in the right hand and when they fall to the ground, whatever number or numbers turn up, they represent the number of holes in the ground, and the first move is made by the first player's "horse" *(ginse)*. The horses are made of any kind of wood, and are of different shapes, so that each man may recognize his own. Every player has his personal stone, which is supposed to bring him luck, and he frequently blows or spits on it. There are also sticks about three feet long with forked ends to pull in the *ginse*.

If the same number is thrown by the second player, the first man's horse is "killed" and has to start over again. When the winning horse has traversed the course, his direction is reversed, then every other player's horse is against him. Should the winner send the other horses to start over, it becomes dangerous for his "pet," therefore he is careful to jump him over the other horses and not kill any of them.

When the leading man is nearing the end, he must be careful of the last hole, called the "fire" *(naada)*, and if on the home stretch he throws number fourteen or fifteen, he "burns up" and is forced to start over again. Anyone going in either direction, if he throws the highest numbers and lands in the first, which is also the last hole, he burns up. The nearest players to the holes move the horses according to the numbers thrown, "but they must be watched, or they might cheat."

In olden times the players sat cross-legged on the ground and could remain in that position for hours. At the court which I saw, the game was shaded by three mesquite trees and there were convenient banks of earth, an old tin tank, a tin toolbox, a milkcan, buckets, etc., for seats. Any number of men, "the more the merrier," came every Sunday afternoon to play.

George Webb told me that bets were made on the players, and sometimes a village elected a contestant to represent it in playing against another community. Nowadays the game is

128

played only for fun and entertainment, not for gain. (See Russell, pp. 175-176; figs. 89, 90; Culin, pp. 148-152, figs. 170-176; Smith.)

● ● ●

"LADIES' GAME"

Informant: Stephen Jones

Two women played this game, using about twelve round stones the size of marbles. One player tossed up a stone and pushed the remaining ones under her cupped left hand before catching the thrown pebble. If she missed it, the other woman took her turn. The score was kept by marks on the ground. Now they use metal "jacks" which "cost fifteen cents a set." (See Russell, p. 179, fig. 94).

● ● ●

RACING GAME

Informant: George Webb

A racing game, called *wee-ichida,* was played, using a ball made of mesquite wood or of a light volcanic stone called *totshak,* which means 'foam on the water.' Both kinds of balls were dipped in boiling mesquite gum *(kwi choovadak),* or creosote gum, and allowed to cool; they were then black, and as smooth as glass. My informant showed me one of the stone balls, which was about eight inches in diameter. A long time ago the men ran and kicked the ball barefoot, but later they wore cowhide sandals. One man raced against another, sometimes for four to five miles and back. Prizes consisted of a cow, a horse, oxen, etc. Occasionally a man would cheat by using four balls, then he was not forced to look for the regular single ball when it flew off into the brush. "Following a kicked ball would make a man go faster, like driving a car," George said.

Lewis Manuel's father used to start early in the morning for Casa Blanca, more than twenty miles distant, kick a ball all the way, and would irrigate his crops and return before night.

In olden days, if a man was very expert with the running-game ball, it was buried with him. (See Russell, pp. 172-174, figs. 87, 88.)

Tarahumara Inidans of Chihuahua are famous runners the world over. Preparatory to their big races they practice by kicking a massive wooden ball as they run. (See Toor, p. 279; Bennett and Zingg, p. 335 et seq.)

● ● ●

VOPODA

Informant: Mason McAffee

Vopoda was played by men at night. A fire of dry wood was made, three men sitting on one side and three on the other. The players first put up prizes, such as their clothes, new pieces of cloth, money, or even women, and bets were made individually between members of the opposing parties.

A player from each side had two small sticks of arrowwood just large enough to be hidden in each hand. One stick was white, the other wound with red cloth. When these were concealed, the players folded their arms and, squatting on their heels, swayed their bodies from side to side. There were three players and three guessers, and a man from the guessing side would concentrate for a while, then clap his hands and indicate the place where the red stick was hidden. If he was successful, his side scored a point and the sticks were passed to the opponents and the procedure was reversed. A scorekeeper was chosen, who cut twenty long sticks, and each time a point was made, one counter was allowed to the winners; when they had won all the sticks, the game was over.

Many people stood about, placed their bets and sang songs, even composing new ones.

130

● ● ●

WOOLEVEGA

Informant: Dean McArthur

Woolevega refers to something tied into a bundle like grain, also sagebrush wrapped in mesquite bark, which was thrown ahead of a marksman for a moving target, according to Father Antonine. Its aim was to become expert at shooting through practice. Long grass, *(Spoolevam)* sour clover *(Melilotus indica L.)*, or tips of *oos hawkmaki* (arrowwood), were cut and folded into one-foot lengths. This bundle was wound round and round with mesquite or willow bark until it was three or four inches thick, when it was ready for use. The *woolevega* was placed about thirty feet away on the ground and several boys, twelve to fourteen years old, used it as a target for their arrows. (Boys at this age were supposed to take up the duties of manhood, such as hunting and protecting the family from the enemy.) The first boy who hit the target picked it up and tossed it into the air, quickly drawing his bow and aiming an arrow at it. He was allowed four shots. If he made a lucky hit, he won all the prizes; but if he lost, the game started over again until a boy hit both the target on the ground and again in the air. At the beginning of the match each youth put up one of his possessions for the prize, such as feathers, arrows, slingshots, sinew, paint, etc. (See Russell, p. 178.)

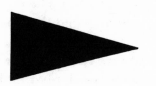

Legends
● ● ●

CORN AND TOBACCO LEGEND (1)

Informant: Domingo Blackwater

The Pima were very fortunate because they arrived in this land where grew tall corn and good tobacco; but all the people had a big quarrel, and for punishment the corn went East, where they say it now grows best, and the tobacco went West. The Pima grabbed some of each, so now they have a little of both.

• • •

CORN AND TOBACCO LEGEND (2)

Informant: Stephen Jones

Tobacco *(viff)* boasted that he was the most important item in smoking, but the Corn *(hoony)* claimed he was still more important, as no tobacco could be smoked without cornhusks.

• • •

HOW RATTLESNAKE GOT ITS FANGS (1)

Informant: Domingo Blackwater

The Creator made the rattlesnake *(kaw-oi)* very beautiful, as it is to this day (if you have noticed), but He gave the serpent nothing with which to protect himself. When the people first came, they played with the snake, rolling him up, throwing and catching him like a ball, and even twisting him around their necks and tying him in a knot.

The snake spoke to his Creator, complaining that he was being tormented and that his ribs ached, and said, "Do something to help me!" The Creator told the serpent to open his mouth, and two fangs were placed in it. The next person who toyed with the rattler was bitten and died within an hour. This news was spread among all the people and they never tried to play with a snake again. (Here the story was cut because it was too long.)

Domingo Blackwater's wife's grandfather would play with snakes and could take a coiled sidewinder into his cupped palm. Some old people were able to do this, because they had no fear, but it cannot be done by those of the younger generation.

• • •

HOW RATTLESNAKE GOT ITS FANGS (2)

Informant: Emma Howard

When appealed to for help, the Creator placed two sun-
beams in the serpent's mouth and they became his fangs.
Not knowing this, the rabbit gave him a scornful kick and was
immediately bitten. The news of the rabbit's death frightened
the people, who ever after have feared and respected the
serpent.

• • •

HOW ROADRUNNER (D'ADAI)
GOT RED ON HIS HEAD

Informant: George Webb

A long time ago an old woman had a pet rattlesnake *(kaw-
oi)*, and when it died she had no fire with which to cremate
her pet. The roadrunner, offering to procure some for her,
flew up to the sun, the journey taking four days. On his return
trip, a thunderstorm arose and lightning struck him right on
the head, but he brought back the fire. That is how the roadrunner got red on his head.

Lewis Manuel's legend of the roadrunner differs from the
above: The bird procured the fire from the sun, and was re-
turning on a trail through the mountains when *wihom* ('the
Lightning Man who shoots' and who is very mean) took his
gun and shot. Because of "the ups and downs" he could hit
the roadrunner on only one side. Lightning Man shot again,
but the mountains prevented the bird from being killed, and
he was just wounded on the other side. That is how the roadrunner got his red markings.

• • •

SAHUARO WINE

Informant: Stephen Jones

A long, long time ago all the birds got together and made sahuaro fruit wine *(ha-ashan navait)*, of which they drank much. A very small bird like a swallow, but larger than a sparrow, became drunk first and fell to the ground. Everyone walked on him and flattened out his head, so that now he is called *komalk maw-okam* ('flat head').

The mockingbird *(shook)* was the next to become drunk. He then began to talk and is still talking.

The whip-poor-will, who has a large mouth, wanted to impress the girls by spitting, and he secretly used a straw for this purpose with great success. The grasshopper *(shaw-o)* was jealous, and, suspecting something, he determined to expose the secret, so he began to dance, hoping to make the whip-poor-will laugh. As he failed in this, the grasshopper, in desperation, finally pulled off one of his legs, put it on his shoulder, and continued dancing. He looked so funny that the bird laughed, the straw fell out, revealing his big mouth. The girls were disgusted and left him. (A small mouth, like long hair, is a sign of beauty among the Pima.)

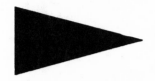

Miscellaneous beliefs
● ● ●

LIGHTNING CURE FOR WARTS

Informant: Stephen Jones

On a threatening day a person afflicted with warts steps out-of-doors, and if lightning strikes, the warts are rubbed off with the palm of the hand. Stephen stated that he thus cured himself three times: once the warts (translated into English as 'pimples') were on his hands, once between his toes, and the third time at the back of his ear.

● ● ●

PLANTING WHEAT

Informant: Stephen Jones

When Stephen Jones was a young fellow, he listened to an old man who was sowing his wheat, long after all other Indians had planted theirs. The old man was repeating: "I throw you down, and in four days you will sprout up"—and it did. He was calling upon a Higher Power for help.

Most Indians had a theory about plant reproduction, although Stephen Jones stated that "the Pima never thought about it." I was unable to procure any information concerning the matter from my informants.

• • •

PROGNOSTICATION

Informants: George Webb and Lewis Nelson

Lewis Nelson says that he had an uncle, his father's brother, who could predict events and happenings. The uncle would arouse the young boys of the household very early every morning and lecture to them until sunrise, when breakfast was served; and again in the evening he would talk to them. Lewis confesses that at the time he lent only half an ear, but when he reached the age of twenty all that he had been told suddenly returned to him and he then marveled at the great wisdom and knowledge of his uncle, whose predictions had come true.

One of the admonitions Lewis still remembers is: "Keep this in mind: never live a shame, but live your life as a good man. Whatever kind of life you live, it will impress and affect the people around you."

George Webb and Lewis Nelson both agree that power flows from certain people and it can be felt at a distance of several feet.

• • •

PROTECTION AGAINST WHIRLWINDS

Informant: Lewis Manuel

Lewis Manuel told me that he has a brother who lives at Casa Blanca and when he sees a whirlwind approaching, he steps out of his house, crosses his index fingers, and hums. With this method he keeps the whirlwind from entering his house, and it just passes by. Sir James George Frazer (pp. 82-83) gives various practices which are employed throughout the world to combat whirlwinds.

The illustrations
● ● ●

The plate *Pimo Women* (on the next page), is from a color seri-
graph which appeared in the original edition and was hand
printed by Louie Ewing, faithfully reproducing a nineteenth
century lithograph printed in Germany.

The black and white photographs interspersed throughout the
text are by:

Odd S. Halseth

R. H. Peebles

C. C. Pierce
   courtesy Southwest Museum

Southwest Museum

PIMO WOMEN

Works consulted
● ● ●

BADIANUS

The Badianus manuscript (*Codex Barberini,* Latin 241) Vatican Library. An Aztec herbal of 1552. Introduction, translation and annotations by Emily Walcott Emmart with a foreword by Henry E. Sigerist, Baltimore. The Johns Hopkins Press. 1940.

BARTLETT, John Russell

Personal narrative of explorations and incidents in Texas, New Mexico, California, Sonora, and Chihuahua . . . during the years 1850, '51, '52, and '53. 2 vols. New York. 1854.

BEAL, Mary

Incense bush. *Desert Magazine,* Vol. 6, No. 8, El Centro, Calif. June 1943.

BENNETT, Wendell C., and ZINGG, Robert M.

The Tarahumara, an Indian tribe of northern Mexico. Chicago. *c.* 1935.

BRYAN, Nonabah G., and YOUNG, Stella

Navajo native dyes, their preparation and use. Recipes formulated by Nonabah G. Bryan, Navajo. Compiled by Stella Young. Illustrated with d r a w i n g s by Charles Keetsie Shirley, Navajo. Chilocco, Okla. 1940.

CASTETTER, Edward F.

Uncultivated native plants used as sources of food. *University of New Mexico Bulletin, Biological series,* Vol. 4, No. 1. Albuquerque. 1935.

CASTETTER, Edward F., and UNDERHILL, Ruth M.

The ethnobiology of the Papago Indians. *University of New Mexico Bulletin, Biological series.* Vol. 4, No. 3. Albuquerque. 1935.

147

CHAMBERLIN, William H.

From Lewisburg to California in 1849. Edited by Lansing B. Bloom. *New Mexico Historical Review*. Vol. xx, Nos. 1-4. Santa Fe. 1945.

CODEX BARBERINI

See BADIANUS.

COLTON, Harold S.

The anatomy of the female American lac insect Tachardiella larrea. Museum of Northern Arizona, *Bulletin 21*. Flagstaff. July 1944.

CULIN, Stewart

Games of the North American Indians. *Twenty-fourth Annual Report Bureau of American Ethnology*, 1902-1903. Washington. 1907.

EMMART, Emily Walcott

Trans. See BADIANUS.

EMORY, W. H.

Notes of a military reconnoissance, from Fort Leavenworth, in Missouri, to San Diego, in California, including parts of the Arkansas, Del Norte, and Gila rivers. Washington. 1848.

FRAZER, James George

The golden bough. Abridged edition. 1 Vol. New York. 1923.

HART, Elizabeth

Pima cookery. Pima Jurisdiction Home Extension Lesson Leaflet Series. Pima Indian Agency. Sacaton, Arizona.

HIGGINS, Ethel Bailey

Our native cacti. New York. 1931.

HOUGH, Walter

The Hopi in relation to their plant environment. *American Anthropologist*, o. s., Vol. x, No. 2, Washington, Feb. 1897.

HOUGH, Walter

Environmental interrelations in Arizona. *American Anthropologist*, o.s., Vol. xi, No. 5. Washington. May 1898.

KEARNEY, Thomas H., and PEEBLES, Robert H.

Flowering plants and ferns of Arizona. *Misc. Pub. 423, U.S. Dept. Agriculture*, Washington. 1942.

MARTINEZ, Maximo

Las plantas medicinales de Mexico. Ediciones Botas, Mexico. 1933.

148

MASON, Otis Tufton — Aboriginal American basketry: studies in a textile art without machinery. *Annual Report U.S. National Museum for 1901-02.* Washington. 1904.

McCLINTOCK, James H. — Arizona, The Youngest State.

PEEBLES, Robert H. — See KEARNEY, Thomas H., and PEEBLES.

RUSSELL, Frank — The Pima Indians. *Twenty-sixth Annual Report Bureau of American Ethnology,* 1904-05. Washington. 1908.

SAUNDERS, Charles Francis — Useful wild plants of the United Stataes and Canada. New York. 1926.

SAUNDERS, Charles Francis — Western wild flowers and their stories. New York. 1933.

SMITH, William Neil, II — The Papago game of "gince goot." *The Masterkey,* Vol. 19, No. 6. Los Angeles. November 1945.

STANDLEY, Paul C. — See WOOTON, E. O., and STANDLEY.

STONE, Eric — Medicine among the American Indians. *Clio medica,* VII. New York. 1932.

TOOR, Frances — A treasury of Mexican folkways. New York. *c.* 1947.

UNDERHILL, Ruth M. — See CASTETTER, Edward F., and UNDERHILL.

WHITING, Alfred F. — Ethnobotany of the Hopi. Museum of Northn Arizona, *Bulletin* No. 15. Flagstaff. June 1939.

WILLENBRINK, Rev. Antonine — Notes on the Pima Indian language. Franciscan Fathers of California. [Santa Barbara, Calif.] *c.* 1935.

WOOTON, E. O., and STANDLEY, Paul C. — Flora of New Mexico. *Contributions from the United States National Herbarium,* Vol. 19. Washington. 1915.

YOUNG, Stella — See BRYAN, N. G., and YOUNG.

ZINGG, R. M. — See BENNETT, W. C., and ZINGG.

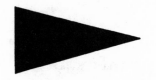

Index

● ● ●

151

153

156

DESIGNED BY MERLE ARMITAGE
DRAWINGS BY GERRI CHANDLER